Eat and Explore

Virginia

D1532014

Eat and Explore
Virginia

Christy Campbell

Great American Publishers
www.GreatAmericanPublishers.com

TOLL-FREE 1-888-854-5954

Great American Publishers

P. O. Box 1305 • Kosciusko, MS 39090

TOLL-FREE 1-888-854-5954 • www.GreatAmericanPublishers.com

ISBN 978-1-934817-12-4 (1-934817-12-0)

First Edition
10 9 8 7 6 5 4 3 2 1

by Christy Campbell

Front Cover Image: Mark P. Anderson, Big Whiskey Design Studio
Back cover image: Stratford Hall
Back cover food image: Chincoteague Island Chamber of Commerce
Chapter opening photos, istockphoto.com: Appetizers & Beverages p9 © Smokingdrum
Soups Salads & Breads p33 © funwithfood • Vegetables & Other Side Dishes p75
© Diana Didyk • Meat & Seafood p119 © Ezhicheg • Desserts & Other Sweets p181
© Edward ONeil Photography • Index p245 © Christine Anderson Photography

Every effort has been made to ensure the accuracy of the information provided
in this book. However, dates, times and locations are subject to change.
Please call or visit websites for up-to-date information before traveling.

To purchase books in quantity for corporate use, incentives, or fundraising,
please call Great American Publishers at 888-854-5954.

Contents

Introduction

When researching states to add to the **EAT & EXPLORE STATE COOKBOOK SERIES**, I learn the basics. I view the state flag, discover the state flower, learn about the state motto and familiarize myself with the state's geography. My favorite part of this process is learning the nickname, which brings me to... Old Dominion. Wow, what an impressive nickname. History, nobility, founding... These are all words that immediately come to mind when thinking of the Old Dominion. I learned quickly the nickname is indeed apt. If the historic homes located throughout the Commonwealth could talk, they would give a lesson of American history unmatched and untold. If the rolling mountains and vast amounts of cultivated land could sing, they would sing a song of eloquence and determination learned from the workers who toiled in the hot Southern sun in the early days of our country's founding. The numerous sites of Civil War battles would recite poetry of both patriotism and sadness in remembrance of the brave soldiers who valiantly fought for their cause.

Along the journey of discovery through Virginia, it occurred to me there could indeed be volumes needed to describe the scenic wonders of this hallowed land. The majesty of the Blue Ridge Mountains is paralleled by the richness of the Chesapeake Bay, and whether you're hiking in the mountains or headed for the beach, one fact is certain... The path along the way is filled with beauty, recreation, Virginian pride and colorful traditions, each born from a history that instantly unifies locals and travelers alike.

Just as I researched the symbols of the Commonwealth of Virginia, I gained insight into the food and drink that is celebrated, year after year. Virginia's natural resources are honored within these pages. Bountiful vineyards, fragrant lavender, wholesome fruits and vegetables, and delicious seafood are the backdrops to the family gatherings, local celebrations and tourist destinations that define the Commonwealth. ***Fall Festival Brunswick Stew, Peach Salsa, Blue Crab Mac-n-Cheese*** and ***Virginia Pulled Pork BBQ*** are welcoming favorites that bring color to any meal. The delicious fare continues with Southern delights such as ***Aunt Myrtle's Chicken, Cheese Fluff, Old-Fashioned Meatloaf*** and ***Cherry Stuffed French Toast***. Which brings me to the most popular part of just about any good cookbook, the desserts. My sweet tooth stayed in high-gear with anticipation of tasting the fabulous desserts recipes that came across my desk day-after-day. ***Catherine's Fresh Apple Cake, Strawberry Pie, Butterscotch Scotchies*** and ***Lavender Cookies*** are just a sampling of the sugary sweets that are a perfect end to a perfect meal.

This year marks the two-year anniversary of my relationship with Great American Publishers. I want to personally thank each and every person I have the good fortune of meeting and working with during these two years. In the vastness of the American economy, I truly believe it is a treasure and a gift to encounter a company who believes in traditional business values and sticks to them. This is what I've found at Great American Publishers. I cannot place a value on the people who make this company what it is, for they are priceless. Brooke Craig, Leann Crapps, Leslie Shoemaker, Diane Adams, Krista Griffin, Nikki Shoemaker and Anita Musgrove are absolutely fearless, and I am gifted with motivation, inspiration and appreciation to simply be in their presence. I don't think I could ever explain to each of these women how knowing them has influenced my life, but I can say today I am a better person because each one of them are in it.

This introduction would be incomplete without a special mention to Ms. Sheena Steadham. Her laughter, spontaneity, tears and grace are something I miss each and every day. Without her this book would not be what it is, and I stand firm in my hope to someday have the opportunity to again work with her on another project. Sheena, endless thanks to you for being an integral part of this book.

Sheila and Roger Simmons welcomed me into their home for a lunch meeting two years ago, and I will remember that day for a lifetime. I had not seen Sheila in several years, however, it was as if no time had passed. Thus began the second chapter of our teamwork, and it's been a fantastic, scary and wonderful ride since. Sheila and Roger, thank you for taking the risk with me and the **EAT & EXPLORE STATE COOKBOOK SERIES** that Spring day. I am forever grateful.

In the meantime, there is a gigantic jumping pillow nestled within Virginia that my cuddly 8 year old son Preston cannot wait to pounce on. Along the way we are going to stop and let my inquisitive 9 year old son Michael climb to the top of a lookout tower to see "what only the birds can see." Of course, the traveling I'm speaking of is so my husband, Michael, can put his toes in the sand along the beach. I love you Guys, the three of you give me stability and strength, every day.

The eloquent Commonwealth of Virginia is the third stop along the way for the **EAT & EXPLORE STATE COOKBOOK SERIES**. The generosity of Virginians I had the privilege of working with is unmatched, and I hope to encounter each of you as we continue on, exploring... Virginia.

Appetizers & Beverages

Autumn Tea

5 cups boiling water
5 individual tea bags
5 cups unsweetened
   apple juice
2 cups cranberry juice

⅓ cup lemon juice
½ cup sugar
¼ teaspoon pumpkin pie
   spice

Pour boiling water over tea bags; cover and steep 8 minutes. Discard tea bags. Add juices, sugar and spice. Stir until sugar is dissolved. Serve warm or over ice.

Dee Kime
BW Country Store

Great Grandma's Punch

8 cups cranberry juice cocktail
1 (6-ounce) can frozen orange juice
1 (6-ounce) can frozen pineapple juice (can use pineapple
   orange)
1 (6-ounce) bottle concentrated lemon juice
2 cups brandy
2 bottles chilled pink champagne

Mix all ingredients and serve. Very nice with an ice ring made of cranberry juice and fresh cranberries. Lemon and orange slices may be added.

Cindy Zook
River District Festival

Ginger Shrub

Served on the farm site, this drink is slightly spicy. It was the 18th century version of Gatorade, keeping workers hydrated while working the fields in the hot summer sun.

1 gallon water	**1 tablespoon ginger**
½ cup vinegar	**1 cup honey**

Mix all ingredients well and refrigerate overnight before serving.

Claude Moore Colonial Farm

Claude Moore Colonial Farm

6310 Georgetown Pike • McLean
703-442-7557 • www.1771.org

The Claude Moore Colonial Farm is a living history museum that portrays family life on a pre-Revolutionary War era working farm. The Claude Moore Colonial Farm organizes interactive educational programs and special events to further the understanding of everyday life and agriculture in 18th century Virginia. Special events may include Dairy Day, Wheat Harvest, Christmas Wassail, as well as seasonal Colonial Market Fairs. The educational programs include Apprenticeship (youth volunteer opportunities for children ages 10-17), Farm Skills Program, ELC/CLE (overnight programs), Colonial Workshops and more. The Farm is the only privately operated U.S. National Park and is managed by the nonprofit organization, Friends of the Claude Moore Colonial Farm, Inc. For information on the Claude Moore Colonial Farm, including programs, events or membership, please call or visit their website .

Mulled Cider

James River State Park's Stamp of Approval

1 gallon apple cider
1 tablespoon whole cloves
3 cinnamon sticks
4 to 6 orange slices
½ cup fresh cranberries

In a large pot, combine all ingredients and bring to boil. Reduce heat and simmer 20 minutes.

James River State Park

James River State Park

104 Green Hill Drive • Gladstone
434-933-4355 • www.virginiastateparks.gov

Known by many as "Virginia's Best Kept Secret," James River State Park is located in the rolling hills of Buckingham County. With 15 miles of hiking, biking or horseback riding trails, 3 fishing ponds, and an opportunity to canoe 8 miles of the James River, this outdoors paradise calls novices and enthusiasts alike. James River State Park offers primitive tent camping, water and electric campsites, equestrian and group camping. Not a camper? The park also offers 2, 3 and 6 bedroom cabins.

Interpretive programs and a full service canoe livery offer enjoyable activities. A Summer Festival is held each year on the third Saturday of July. The Fall Festival and Haunted Wagon Ride, also an annual event, is held on the third Saturday of October.

Mulled Lavender Cider

1 cup water
1 tablespoon culinary lavender buds
1 gallon organic natural apple cider
1 (48-ounce) bottle apricot juice
1 cinnamon stick

Bring water to boil. Add lavender buds and steep 16 to 20 minutes. Strain; discard lavender buds. Add lavender tea to slow cooker. Add apple cider, apricot juice and cinnamon stick. Stir well and heat on low.

White Oak Lavender Farm

Christmas Wassail

1 bottle sweet red wine (best with MountainRose Vineyard's
  Pardee Red Wine)
1 (64-ounce) bottle apple juice
½ cup sugar
3 tablespoons mulling spices in bag
Orange or lemon slices, optional

Combine wine, juice, sugar and spice in crockpot. Add orange or lemon slices, if desired, 10 minutes before serving. Serve very warm.

MountainRose Vineyard • www.mountainrosevineyard.com
Wise County Famous Fall Fling

Super Peach Smoothie

1½ cups peeled and chopped fresh peaches (frozen may be
   substituted)
2 tablespoons flax seed or wheat germ
1 stalk kale
Orange juice
1 cup plain yogurt, optional

Place all ingredients in blender and process until it reaches
desired consistency. Serve immediately.

Amanda Wingfield, Patrick County Extension Office
Virginia State Peach Festival

Super Fruity Lite Sangria

1 bottle red wine (best with
   MountainRose Vineyard's
   Pardee Red)
1 lemon, cut into wedges
1 lime, cut into wedges
1 orange, cut into wedges

1 peach, cut into wedges
1 cup sliced strawberries
½ cup lemonade or limeade
½ cup sugar
2 cups ginger ale

Pour wine into pitcher and squeeze in juice from lemon, lime
and orange wedges; reserve wedges in airtight container. Chill
overnight. Add peach slices, strawberries, lemonade/limeade,
saved fruit wedges and sugar about ½ hour before serving in
large punch bowl. Add ginger ale and a punch ring or ice just
before serving.

MountainRose Vineyard • www.mountainrosevineyard.com
Wise County Famous Fall Fling

Buffalo Chicken Dip

1 pound cooked chicken
2 (8-ounce) packages cream cheese, softened
10 ounces buffalo hot wing sauce
8 ounces shredded Cheddar cheese, divided

Combine chicken, cream cheese, hot wing sauce and ½ cheese. Bake at 350° for 25 minutes. Top with remaining cheese. Cook an additional 5 minutes or until cheese bubbles. Serve with celery, corn chips or other chips.

Sara Dickey
River District Festival

River District Festival

October

Danville River District
434-799-2166
www.riverdistrictfestival.org

The Danville Area Association for the Arts & Humanities and the Danville Regional Foundation partner with community agencies, local businesses and organizations to host a day long festival to celebrate the arts and increase awareness and visibility of the River District. Events include a children's festival, river educational activities, musical entertainment provided by local and national performers, art shows, arts and crafts vendors, food and beverage vendors and a showcase of local businesses and organizations. Visit their website for details on each year's event details.

Black Bean Dip

2 (15-ounce) cans black beans,
   drained and rinsed
¼ cup lime juice
1 garlic clove
2 tablespoons olive oil

1 teaspoon cumin
½ teaspoon onion powder
⅛ teaspoon red pepper
¼ teaspoon salt

Place all ingredients in food processor and blend until smooth.
Serve with favorite chips, crackers or fresh veggies.

Abingdon Medical Museum

Abingdon Medical Museum

228 West Valley Street • Abingdon
276-206-8691 • www.abingdonmedicalmuseum.com
Hours: Mon – Fri, 10am to 2pm; Sat – Sun, 10am to 3pm

Established by Dr. Damian Sooklal, Abingdon Medical Museum is a must-see for anyone visiting the beautiful Historic District of Abingdon. This distinctive museum appeals to visitors of all ages with exhibits of medical artifacts from the early nineteenth century up to present day with a focus on the history of medicine, especially as it relates to southwest Virginia. Housed in a 110-year-old building built by a Civil War veteran who later became a member of the Virginia House of Delegates, it's unique learning environment demonstrates the importance of early medical artifacts to our past and present. By preserving medical artifacts and sharing them through museum exhibits and other events, we hope to provide the general public with a better understanding of health care issues and to stimulate young people to careers in science and medicine all in a way that enriches the cultural environment of the region.

Sun-Dried Tomato with Goat Cheese Dip

1 (8-ounce) package cream cheese, softened
8 to 12 ounces goat cheese
2 tablespoons milk

Blend all ingredients. Spread into mound on plate. (Makes enough to cover a 12-inch dinner plate.)

Topping:
1 to 3 garlic cloves
¼ cup fresh basil
¼ cup fresh parsley
1 tablespoon olive oil
¼ teaspoon Italian seasoning
Salt and pepper to taste
8 to 10 ounces sun-dried tomatoes, chopped
   (drain and reserve oil)

Combine garlic, basil, parsley, oil, Italian seasoning, salt and pepper in a food processor and blend well. Scoop into bowl, add sun-dried tomatoes and mix thoroughly. Use reserved oil for desired consistency. Pour mixture evenly over cheese mound; refrigerate overnight. Serve with sliced baguettes or crackers.

Roseann Walling, Maymont Special Events Coordinator
Herbs Galore & More at Maymont

Peach Salsa

1 cup sliced fresh peaches (may substitute with frozen)
1 tablespoon chopped fresh parsley
¼ teaspoon ground cinnamon
2 tablespoons orange juice
½ tablespoon seeded and chopped jalapeño pepper, optional

Combine all ingredients in food processor and process until well blended; chill. Serve with tortilla chips.

Amanda Wingfield, Patrick County Extension Office
Virginia State Peach Festival

Virginia State Peach Festival

August

**Stuart DeHart Park
   and Meadows of Dan
Stuart
276-694-6012
www.patrickchamber.com**

The Patrick County Chamber of Commerce hosts the Virginia State Peach Festival each summer during August. First held on August 10, 1988 on the farm of Mr. J .P. Via, the festival featured fresh peaches, homemade peach cobbler, peach ice cream and peach wine coolers. It has grown tremendously since its first gathering and holds the title "Peach Festival of Virginia."

The weekend celebration includes the Virginia State Peach Pageant, a music celebration on Friday night, bushels of ripe peaches, art and craft exhibits, and the Folk Fair on Saturday at the Meadows of Dan. Of course, the ice cream, wine coolers and cobblers are still there.

Fruit Salsa & Chips

1 cup cored and chopped
    strawberries
2 medium kiwi
1 medium orange

1 (8-ounce) can crushed
    pineapple, drained
1 tablespoon lemon juice

Wash, peel and chop all fruit. Combine in bowl and chill 6 hours.
Serve with Baked Cinnamon Tortilla Chips.

Baked Cinnamon Tortilla Chips:

12 (8-inch) flour tortillas
1 stick butter, melted

½ cup sugar
1 tablespoon cinnamon

Slice each tortilla into 8 triangle-shaped pieces (like cutting a
pizza). Brush with butter. Mix sugar and cinnamon together
and sprinkle over tortillas. Bake at 350° for 5 to 10 minutes until
dry and lightly browned.

Occoquan Craft Fair

Patrick County

Experience the Simple Life

Travel back to a time when arts and crafts
were a necessity for daily living. Whether picking
cherries, peaches or apples, exploring the intricate
paths of a corn maze, taking a walk along the
hiking and birding trails at Fairy Stone State Park,
Rock Castle Gorge, or IC Dehart Park, hidden treasures
are waiting to be discovered in this tranquil area. Wind down The Crooked Road,
Virginia's Heritage Music Trail or enjoy a scenic drive on the Blue Ridge Parkway.
www.visitpatrickcounty.org • www.patrickchamber.com

Guacamole Dip

2 medium avocados
1 tablespoon minced jalapeño pepper
2 tablespoons minced cilantro
Juice ½ fresh lime
Salt and pepper to taste
¼ cup salsa

Spoon out avocado meat and mash with fork. Add remaining ingredients and mix well. Serve immediately with tortilla chips.

Candice's Taco Dip

2 (8-ounce) packages cream cheese, softened
1 (16-ounce) carton sour cream
1 tablespoon milk
1 tablespoon Worcestershire sauce
1 package dry taco seasoning
Lettuce, grated cheese, tomatoes, olives and onions for topping

Combine first 4 ingredients and blend until smooth. Layer onto pizza pan. Sprinkle with taco seasoning and top with toppings. Chill until serving time. Serve with tortilla chips.

Candice Slater
Virginia Southern Gospel Jubilee

Mustard Dip

1 cup spicy brown mustard
¼ cup sour cream
2 tablespoons horseradish

Combine all ingredients and mix well. Serve with miniature sausage bites.

Liberty Mountain Snowflex

Liberty Mountain Snowflex Centre

4000 Candlers Mountain Road • Lynchburg
434-582-3539 • www.liberty.edu/snowflex

The Liberty Mountain Snowflex Centre, located in the Piedmont community of Lynchburg, boasts the only year-round skiing, snowboarding, and tubing facility in the United States. Because of the unique Snowflex material, which mimics the grip and slip action of real snow, riders from across the country come to hone their skills regardless of the weather! It also features the two-story Barrick-Falwell Lodge, known for its rustic beauty and breathtaking views. Here guests can rent

equipment, sign up for lessons, or simply enjoy the cozy upper lodge and refreshments from concessions. The Lodge is available to rent for events ranging from children's birthday parties to wedding receptions and business meetings. The Liberty Mountain Snowflex Centre hosts regional and national competitions throughout the year, drawing in competitors from the U.S. as well as Canada and beyond.

Hot Virginia Dip

1 cup chopped pecans
1 teaspoon butter
2 (8-ounce) packages cream cheese, softened
4 teaspoons milk

5 ounces dried beef (2 small jars)
1 teaspoon garlic salt
1 cup sour cream
4 teaspoons minced onion

Preheat oven to 350°. Sauté pecans in butter; set aside. In a separate bowl combine remaining ingredients and mix well. Pour in 1½-quart baking dish and top with pecans. Bake 20 minutes. Serve hot with crackers.

Jane Barnes, Executive Director
Blackstone Chamber of Commerce
Blackstone Arts & Crafts Festival

Blackstone Arts & Crafts Festival

Second Weekend in September

Corner of Tavern and High Streets
Blackstone
434-292-1677
www.blackstoneva.com

For over four decades, the Blackstone Chamber of Commerce has sponsored the Blackstone Arts & Crafts Festival. The Historic District livens up every year in September, featuring unique artwork, eye-catching crafts, delicious food, petting zoo, Kids Zone, live entertainment, an

antique tractor and classic car show, Civil War re-enactment, wine tasting and a 5K run/walk. This free festival draws approximately 4,000 visitors every year.

Blackstone offers many other fun events. Bevell's Hardware Giant Train Display, the Classic Car Cruise In, the Hometown Jams Concert Series, Christmas Open House with Grand Illumination, and numerous restaurants. Visit their site for details on these events.

Spinach Dip

1 cup mayonnaise
1 cup sour cream
1 package Knorr Spring Vegetable Mix
1 (10-ounce) package frozen spinach
2 cups shredded Cheddar cheese, divided

Preheat oven to 350°. In a glass or ceramic pie plate mix together mayonnaise, sour cream and vegetable mix. Cook spinach as directed and squeeze out liquid. Add to mixture and blend well. Stir in 1 cup cheese and spread evenly. Top with remaining cheese. Cook 30 minutes or until cheese browns around edges. Serve immediately with tortilla chips.

Grace McDonald
Blackstone Arts & Crafts Festival

Virginia Apple Dip

1 (8-ounce) package cream cheese, softened
½ cup brown sugar
¼ cup white sugar
1 teaspoon vanilla extract
1 (8-ounce) package toffee baking bits

Blend cream cheese, sugars and vanilla. Add toffee. Mix well and serve with apple slices.

Pumpkin Dessert Dip

1 (8-ounce) package cream cheese, softened
1 (7-ounce) jar marshmallow creme
½ cup canned pumpkin
¼ teaspoon cinnamon
¼ teaspoon nutmeg

Combine all ingredients. Mix until well blended. Cover and refrigerate 4 hours. Serve with graham crackers, vanilla wafers, shortbread or fruit.

Culpeper Air Fest

Hampton Bay Days Hot Crab Dip

1 (8-ounce) package cream cheese, softened
½ cup sour cream
2 tablespoons mayonnaise
1 tablespoon lemon juice
1¼ teaspoons Worcestershire sauce
½ teaspoon dry mustard
Pinch garlic salt
1 tablespoon milk
¼ cup grated Cheddar cheese, divided
½ pound Graham & Rollins Crabmeat (available in Hampton of course!)

In large bowl, mix cream cheese, sour cream, mayonnaise, lemon juice, Worcestershire sauce, mustard and garlic salt until smooth. Add milk. Add 2 tablespoons cheese. Fold crabmeat into cream cheese mixture. Pour into greased 1-quart casserole. Top with remaining cheese. Bake at 325° for 30 minutes or until browned. Serve with crackers. Perfect for enjoying during Hampton Bay Days' fireworks.

Hampton Bay Days

Hampton Bay Days

September

Downtown Hampton
757-727-1641
800-800-2202
www.baydays.com

This annual festival combines entertainment on multiple stages, family friendly activity areas with children's stage, 100 arts and crafts booths, 35 food vendors and one of the longest fireworks displays in the area. An estimated

200,000 fun seekers and festival attendees attend Bay Days annually.

One of the event highlights is the Bay Education and Children's Area. Bringing awareness to Chesapeake Bay, one of the state's most important natural resources (and the nation's largest estuary), this area features over 20 interactive booths on environmentalism, conservationism and clean water. Both festival and musical entertainment admissions are free. Boaters are invited to dock and enjoy the festivities.

Lumpia

This egg roll is fun to make. You can use all kinds of different ingredients. Enjoy lumpia made of chicken, ground beef, pork, shrimp or just your favorite vegetables! The combinations are endless.

2 pounds ground beef
2 teaspoons black pepper, divided
¼ cup chopped garlic, divided
¼ cup chopped onions, divided
1 cup chopped carrots
1 cup cubed potatoes

1 cup chopped water chestnuts
2 teaspoons soy sauce
Salt to taste
Canola oil for frying
Lumpia wrappers (frozen egg roll
    wraps found at Asian grocery)

The meat should be browned in a large skillet. Add 1 teaspoon black pepper and half the garlic and onions, mixing well; drain. Add remaining garlic and onions. Add carrots, potatoes and water chestnuts and cook until tender. Add remaining black pepper, soy sauce and salt; mix well. Remove from heat and allow to cool thoroughly. Drop 2 tablespoons filling onto lumpia wrapper. Starting from corner, roll tightly and neatly around filling, folding and tucking edges. Seal edge with water. Pour enough canola oil in fry pan for deep frying and heat over medium-high heat. Deep fry lumpia rolls until golden brown. Drain on paper towel. Serve with sweet and sour sauce or your favorite sauce.

Filipino Festival

Filipino Festival

Our Lady of Lourdes Catholic Church
8200 Woodman Road
Richmond
804-262-7315
www.filipinofestival.org

Mabuhay! Held the second weekend in August, the Annual Filipino Festival is a community-wide event which showcases the Filipino culture and heritage. Attendees enjoy traditional dance, music and song with delectable cuisine such as lumpia, halo-halo, adobo, pancit, San Miguel beer and more. With its hallmark of food and entertainment, the popular Annual Filipino Festival continues to attract thousands of attendees and is probably one of the largest Filipino Festivals in the United States.

The party starts on Friday night when several popular local bands take the stage. The Festival features children's games, exhibits, crafts, jewelry, clothing, health screenings and many vendors. Admission is free. The Festival is sponsored by Our Lady of Lourdes Catholic Church, and proceeds benefit local food pantries, clothes closets, scholarships, and the Lakeside Free Clinic.

Come celebrate the richness of the Philippines without leaving Virginia!

Party Rolls

1 tablespoon Worcestershire
½ small onion, finely chopped
2 sticks butter, softened
2 tablespoons prepared mustard
3 tablespoons poppy seeds
3 packages Pepperidge Farms Party Rolls, frozen
1 pound shredded sharp cheese
1 pound chopped country ham

Combine Worcestershire, onion, butter, mustard and poppy seed; set aside. Carefully slice entire packages frozen rolls through center, making 2 6-bread halves. Do not break apart rolls. Spread mixture evenly on all bread halves. Sprinkle cheese evenly over bottom halves and ham on other half. Close sandwiches. Tightly wrap rolls in aluminum foil and thaw 30 minutes. Place on cookie sheet and bake at 350° for 20 to 30 minutes. Separate rolls and serve.

Culpeper Air Fest

Fall Festival of Folklife

Just Right Deviled Eggs

12 eggs, boiled and peeled
4 tablespoons mayonnaise
2 tablespoons mustard

¼ teaspoon salt
¼ teaspoon pepper
Paprika

Cut eggs in half lengthwise. Gently remove yolks and put in bowl; set whites aside. Mash yolks and add mayonnaise, mustard, salt and pepper. Spoon yolk mixture into hollowed egg whites. Sprinkle with paprika.

Fall Festival of Folklife

Fall Festival of Folklife

October

Newport News Park
757-926-1400
www.nnparks.com

The Newport News Fall Festival of Folklife is southeastern Virginia's biggest traditional craft show. The festival features a crafts competition for the highest skilled craftspeople and a demonstration area where attendees can see the creation of items from raw natural materials to the finished craft product.

The Fall Festival of Folklife is more than just a craft show... It is a celebration of folklife traditions that have been passed down through the generations. The entertainment stages are filled with folk dancing, bluegrass, country, and folk music. Children can make-and-take their own crafts and meet farm animals. Of course no one can resist stopping for snacks when the air is filled with the scent of kettle corn, freshly cooked park rinds, barbeque, seafood, and roasted corn on the cob. The festivities are highlighted in the beautiful wooded area along the lake in the 8,000-acre Newport News Park.

Piquant Cheese Tea Sandwich

10 ounces extra sharp Cheddar cheese, grated
1 small onion, finely grated
1 small green bell pepper, finely chopped
Dash cayenne pepper
2 to 3 dashes Worcestershire sauce
Ketchup

Mix together cheese, onion and pepper. Add cayenne pepper and Worcestershire sauce. Add just enough ketchup to make cheese spreadable. Use with any variety of thin bread.

Hunter House Victorian Museum

Spiced Nuts

½ teaspoon ground coriander
½ teaspoon ground cumin
3 tablespoons butter
2 tablespoons brown sugar
1½ teaspoons Worcestershire sauce

½ teaspoon cayenne pepper
1½ teaspoons salt
3 cups pecans
1 cup shelled pistachios
2 cups almonds

Preheat oven to 325°. In skillet over low heat, combine coriander, cumin, butter, sugar, Worcestershire sauce, cayenne and salt. Cook slowly until butter melts and sugar dissolves. Keep warm. Place nuts on baking sheet. Bake 10 to 15 minutes, shaking several times. Put nuts in bowl and drizzle butter mixture until well coated. Cool completely.

Very Virginia Shop

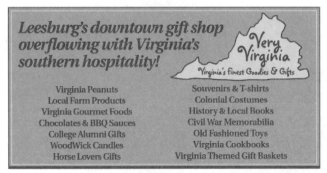

Herb De Provence

2 tablespoons lavender
2 tablespoons rosemary
2 tablespoons marjoram
2 tablespoons basil

2 tablespoons thyme
2 tablespoons savory
2 tablespoons oregano
2 tablespoons garlic powder

Blend all herbs and store in airtight container. Use as favorite seasoning.

White Oak Lavender Farm

White Oak Lavender Farm

5060 Newcomer Lane • Harrisonburg
540-421-6345 • www.whiteoaklavender.com

White Oak Lavender is a family owned lavender farm in Harrisonburg. Over 7,000 lavender plants are grown on the farm in fragrant whites, pinks, blues and purples. Some are sweet culinary varieties and others are used for their deep bodied scent and essential oils. The farm is open year round as an agri-tourism venue. Their mission is to provide

education about the wonderful properties of lavender for relieving stress and healing the skin. They have a delightful shop where they sell their handcrafted bath and body products, sewn lavender pillows, lovely lavender linens and gourmet food products. Daily tours are given in season and classes are offered throughout the year. It is especially fun to watch the distilling demonstrations! Their volunteer harvest days are well attended and much enjoyed by visitors.

Soups, Salads & Breads

Spring Minestrone Soup

2 quarts vegetable broth
2 pounds fresh Roma tomatoes, diced
4 garlic cloves, finely chopped
2 pounds fingerling potatoes, cut into ¾-inch chunks
1 pound artichoke hearts, chopped
2 (15-ounce) cans chick peas
4 tablespoons extra virgin olive oil
12 green onions, chopped
2 cups green peas
1 pound asparagus, cut into ¾-inch chunks
Salt and pepper to taste

In a large pot, combine vegetable broth, tomatoes, garlic and potatoes. Simmer 15 minutes. Add artichoke hearts and chickpeas, simmering an additional 10 minutes. Add olive oil, green onions, green peas and asparagus, cooking 15 minutes over medium heat. Season with salt and pepper.

Chef Jason Smith
Preston's Restaurant, Blacksburg
Blacksburg Fork and Cork

Farmers Market Butternut Squash Soup

¼ cup unsalted butter
1 large yellow onion, chopped
2 celery stalks, chopped
2 medium carrots, chopped
2 thyme springs, leaves stripped
4 medium potatoes, cubed

2 medium butternut squash, peeled, seeded, and cubed
2 (32-ounce) cans chicken stock, divided
¼ cup heavy cream
Salt and pepper to taste

Melt butter in large pot. Cook onion, celery, carrot, thyme, potatoes and squash 5 minutes or until lightly browned. Pour just enough chicken stock to cover vegetables. Bring to a boil. Reduce heat to low, cover and simmer 40 minutes, or until vegetables are tender. Transfer soup to blender and blend until smooth. Return to pot, and mix in remaining stock and heavy cream. Season with salt and pepper.

Chef Randall Spencer
Blue Ridge Mountain Catering
Blacksburg Fork and Cork

Blacksburg Fork and Cork

April

First and Main Shopping District
540-443-2008
www.blacksburgforkandcork.com

blacksburg
FORK
AND CORK

The Blacksburg Partnership hosts the Blacksburg Fork and Cork each spring in beautiful Blacksburg. This food, wine, and art festival began in 2009 and typically is held the last Saturday in April. The day is filled with wine from premier Virginia wineries, art from regional crafters, and delicious food from top local restaurants. Cooking demonstration tents with skilled area chefs will summon the foodie in all of us, and opportunities abound to learn more about the beverage of the day in the many available wine seminars. A fun canned food sculpture contest and food drive is also held each year, benefitting local food pantries.

Classic Southern Tomato Bisque

1 onion, diced
½ cup fresh garlic
½ cup fresh dry basil
¼ cup fresh dry oregano
Bay leaves, crushed
3 cans plum tomatoes

2 cans tomato paste
½ cup sugar
3 to 4 tablespoons chicken base
2 quarts heavy cream
1 tablespoon salt
1 tablespoon pepper

Sauté onion until tender without browning; add garlic, dry herbs, and crushed bay leaves. Sauté 1 minute. Add tomatoes, tomato paste, sugar, chicken base and water for desired consistency. Bring to a simmer. Add heavy cream, salt and pepper. Puree and strain. Serve immediately.

Executive Chef Tony Dellorso
Blackstone Grill, Christiansburg
Blacksburg Fork and Cork

French Onion Soup with Wine

Delicious paired with MountainRose Vineyard's Imboden wine.

2 sticks butter
2 to 3 large sweet onions, chopped
3 tablespoons flour
3 (14½-ounce) cans beef broth
2 (14½-ounce) cans chicken broth
½ cup white wine (best with MountainRose
   Vineyard's Imboden wine)

Melt butter over medium-high in skillet and sauté onions until rich, dark brown. Sprinkle with flour and stir. Add broths and bring to boil; mixture will begin to thicken. Reduce heat to simmer and add wine. Do not boil once wine is added. Serve with crusty chunks of French bread with melted Mozzarella cheese.

MountainRose Vineyard • www.mountainrosevineyard.com
Wise County Famous Fall Fling

French Onion Soup

¼ cup butter
4 yellow onions, peeled and
   chopped
1 teaspoon sugar
4 cups beef broth
1 (12-ounce) bottle favorite
   stout beer
2 teaspoons salt
½ teaspoon dried thyme
1 teaspoon black pepper
4 slices French bread
4 slices Swiss cheese

Blacksburg Fork and Cork

Heat butter in 4-quart Dutch oven over medium-low heat; add onions. Cook, stirring occasionally, 30 minutes or until onions are very soft. Add sugar; continue cooking, stirring often, until onions are golden brown, about 15 minutes. Add broth, beer, salt, thyme and pepper. Increase heat to medium-high; bring mixture to a boil. Reduce heat to low; simmer 30 minutes. Preheat oven to 350°. Place bread on baking sheet. Bake 15 minutes, turning once, until toasted. Preheat broiler. Spoon soup into ovenproof soup bowls. Place bread slice in each bowl; top with cheese. Broil about 4 inches from heat until cheese is melted.

Chef Randall Spencer
Blue Ridge Mountain Catering
Blacksburg Fork and Cork

Cool Cantaloupe Soup with Basil Cream

1 cantaloupe, cut into 1-inch
    chunks
2 tablespoons fresh lemon juice
¼ teaspoon fresh lemon zest
2 tablespoons chopped mint
    leaves

⅛ teaspoon salt
1 cup heavy cream
2 tablespoons sugar
½ cup packed basil leaves
¾ cup champagne

Place cantaloupe, lemon juice and zest in food processor and pulse until roughly chopped. Add mint leaves and salt and pulse to combine. Pour into large bowl, cover and chill 30 minutes. While cantaloupe is chilling, combine cream and sugar in food processor and process until slightly thickened. Add basil and process until thick, about 20 seconds. Set aside. Add champagne to soup right before serving. Divide soup evenly among 4 bowls and top with cream.

Chef Shawn Lawson
Virginia Cantaloupe Festival

Virginia Cantaloupe Festival

July

Halifax County Fairgrounds
South Boston, Virginia
434-572-3085 • 888-458-1003
www.valopefest.com

It's a party going on! A giant party—the fantastic Virginia Cantaloupe Festival held in Halifax County! Over thirty years of hot fun in the summer sun—swaying to the sounds of music drifting across a lush, green carpet; sipping the finest beverages; wiping the juice from a succulent cantaloupe dripping from your chin; feasting on food prepared on site. Admission for this one day, annual event includes music, BBQ, homemade cole slaw, locally grown corn on the cob, fresh tomatoes, vanilla ice cream, fresh fruit cups, beverages and of course, the star of the show—the famous Halifax County cantaloupe.

Don't miss the party!

Shelia Bradley

Zuppa Toscana

1 pound Italian sausage, mild
1¼ teaspoons crushed red pepper
4 slices bacon, cut into ½-inch
   pieces
1 large yellow onion, diced

1 tablespoon minced garlic
5 cups chicken broth
6 Yukon potatoes, thinly sliced
1 cup heavy cream
¼ bunch fresh baby spinach

Cook sausage and red pepper flakes in Dutch oven over medium-high heat until crumbly and brown; drain and set aside. Place bacon in same Dutch oven and cook until crisp; drain, reserving 2 tablespoons bacon drippings in Dutch oven. Stir in onions and garlic. Cook 5 minutes or until onions are soft and translucent. Pour chicken broth into Dutch oven with bacon and onion mixture; bring to a boil. Add potatoes and boil until tender. Reduce heat to medium and stir in heavy cream and cooked sausage; heat through. Mix spinach into soup just before serving.

Chef Randall Spencer
Blue Ridge Mountain Catering
Blacksburg Fork and Cork

Quick Borsch

1 large onion, diced
3 celery stalks, sliced
3 carrots, sliced
1 cup shredded cabbage
2 garlic cloves, minced
2 (14-ounce) cans beef or
   chicken broth

8 cups water
1 package onion soup mix
2 cans beets, grated, with liquid
3 teaspoons ketchup
2 teaspoons parsley
2 teaspoons chives
Salt and pepper to taste

Cook onions, celery, carrots, cabbage and garlic in broth, water and dry soup mix over medium heat 20 minutes. Add grated beets. Cook additional 15 minutes. Add ketchup, parsley, chives, salt and pepper to taste.

Lieda Boyko
International Children's Festival

International Children's Festival

Borscht

Borscht is probably the most famous traditional Russian food and is not only very tasty, but healthy as well.

1 pound beef brisket
1 cup baby carrots
1 cup leeks
½ cup parsley
2 medium onions, chopped
   (divided)
5 to 10 white peppercorns, crushed
2 bay leaves
2 quarts water
Salt to taste
2 medium beets, peeled and sliced
1 tablespoon vinegar, divided
4 tablespoons butter

¾ pound white cabbage, sliced
5 medium potatoes, boiled and
   chopped
4 tablespoons cooked kidney beans
3 tomatoes, chopped
¼ pound cooked ham
3 tablespoons flour
3 garlic cloves
2 tablespoons bacon fat
1 sprig parsley, chopped
1 sprig dill, chopped
Sour cream for garnish

Prepare broth using brisket, vegetables, 1 chopped onion, peppercorns, bay leaves, water and salt. Simmer 1½ hours; strain, reserving liquid. Set aside brisket and vegetables. Braise beets in fat skimmed from broth, season with salt and ½ tablespoon vinegar. Add reserved liquid to cover and simmer until cooked. Chopped reserved vegetables and sauté with remaining onion in butter. In separate saucepan, cover cabbage with reserved liquid and simmer 30 minutes. Add beets, vegetables, onion, potatoes, kidney beans, tomatoes and ham. Simmer until cooked thoroughly. Mix flour and ½ cup reserved liquid in a separate bowl. Slowly add to borscht, mixing in thoroughly. Crush garlic with bacon fat and chopped parsley. Add to soup and steep 15 minutes. Chop brisket into small pieces and add to soup. Season with salt, remaining vinegar and dill. Serve hot with 1 tablespoon sour cream on each helping.

Tatayana Babakaeva
Representative for Russia, International Children's Festival

Buckland Farm Market

Gazpacho

2 cups chopped tomatoes
1 cup finely chopped green bell pepper
1 cup finely chopped celery
1 cup finely chopped cucumber
½ cup finely chopped onion
2 small garlic cloves, minced
4 teaspoons chopped parsley
5 tablespoons balsamic vinegar
1 teaspoon Worcestershire sauce
4 tablespoons olive oil
2 teaspoons cumin
2 teaspoons salt
½ teaspoon pepper
1 cup V-8 juice
4 cups tomato juice
1 can beef consommé
Hot sauce to taste, optional
Sour cream for garnish
Chives for garnish

Combine all ingredients except garnish ingredients. Chill thoroughly and serve in chilled cups or bowls. Top with sour cream and sprinkle with chives.

Margaret
Buckland Farm Market

Taco Soup

1½ to 2 pounds ground beef,
  browned and drained
1 small onion, chopped
1 can whole-kernel corn, drained
1 can pinto beans
1 can navy or great northern beans
1 can kidney beans

2 cans Rotel Tomatoes (diced
  tomatoes with green chilis)
¼ teaspoon salt
1 package taco seasoning mix
1 package ranch dressing mix
1 cup water

Combine all ingredients in large pot over medium-high heat. Bring to a boil, lower heat and simmer approximately 30 minutes. Delicious served over tortilla chips or cornbread.

Tazewell County Airport Airshow

Tazewell County Airport Airshow

2200 Airport Road • Cedar Bluff
276-963-4509 • 276-963-3644

The Tazewell County Airport is a regional airport located in the picturesque mountains of Southwestern Virginia. The airport serves the citizens of Tazewell, Russell and Buchanon counties with such services as Medical related flights, aircraft refueling, utility operations, conference room rentals, charter flights as well as flight instruction.

The airfield hosts the Tazewell County Airshow. Come early for a day of family entertainment and fun. Bring a lawn chair, a straw hat and camera and enjoy local entertainment, static aircraft displays (WAR BIRDS), motion simulators and a variety of food vendors. The Aerobatic Routine will amaze viewers with precision jumps by professional skydivers. Airplane and helicopter rides are available at a reasonable price. Come year after year to discover new acts are added each year along with your favorite performers.

Autumn Harvest Stew

1 pound boneless pork shoulder
2 medium sweet potatoes, peeled and cubed
2 medium white potatoes, peeled and cubed
2 small cooking apples, cored, cut into ¼-inch slices
1 medium onion, chopped
¾ teaspoon crushed dried thyme
½ teaspoon crushed dried rosemary
½ teaspoon salt
¼ teaspoon pepper
2 cups apple cider or apple juice

Trim fat from meat. Cut meat into 1-inch cubes. In a 3½- or 4-quart crockery cooker, layer potatoes, apples and onion. Sprinkle with thyme, rosemary, salt and pepper. Add meat. Pour apple cider or juice over top. Cover and cook on low heat 7 to 8 hours or high heat 3½ to 4 hours.

Grace McDonald
Main Street Framing

Fall Festival Brunswick Stew

Recipe makes 30 gallons of stew over an open fire.

4 gallons water
2 pounds fat meat
2 pounds beef fat
5 stalks celery, chopped
5 pounds carrots, chopped
2 heads cabbage, chopped
4 pounds green bell pepper, chopped
5 pounds onion, chopped
20 pounds cooked turkey (meat picked off bone)
5 pounds cooked pork
4 (104-ounce) cans corn
6 (104-ounce) cans crushed tomatoes
3 (108-ounce) cans butterbeans
3 (104-ounce) cans new potatoes
2 small bottles Worcestershire sauce
2 pounds sugar
1 pound salt
Pepper, garlic and red cayenne pepper to taste

Secret to success — stir constantly and do not stop. In 30 gallon cast-iron pot, add water, fat meat and beef fat; bring to boil. Add celery, carrots, cabbage, bell pepper and onion. Cook 1 hour. Add turkey and pork; boil 1 hour. Add corn and heat to boiling. Add tomatoes and cook 1 hour. Add butterbeans, potatoes, Worcestershire, sugar and salt; lower fire to simmer. Simmer 1 hour. Add seasonings and serve.

Friends of James River State Park
James River State Park

Fish Stew

3 tablespoons olive oil
1 onion, thinly sliced
½ cup chopped celery
Freshly ground salt to taste
1 teaspoon dried thyme
2 garlic cloves, finely chopped
½ cup sliced mushrooms
Pinch cayenne pepper
½ cup roux for thickening, optional
1 (14-ounce) can chopped tomatoes
½ cup dry white wine
6 cups fish stock
½ pound skinless white fish fillets, cut into pieces (cod, grouper, halibut, monk, haddock)
1 pound mussels (scrub fresh mussels well)
½ pound shrimp, peeled and deveined
Saffron water, optional
2 tablespoons fresh parsley or basil, chopped

Heat olive oil in large heavy Dutch oven. Add onion, celery, salt and thyme. Cook on medium-low heat 10 minutes or until onions are tender. Add garlic, mushrooms and cayenne; cook 1 minute. Add roux if desired. Stir in chopped tomatoes, wine and fish stock. Bring to boil for 2 minutes, reduce heat and simmer gently 15 minutes. Add fish to mixture, stirring gently. Simmer over low heat about 3 minutes. Add mussels and shrimp; simmer 2 additional minutes. (If using fresh mussels, simmer until they open. Discard any that remain closed.) Stir in saffron water (if desired), basil and parsley. Great served with a slice of thick bread.

Roya Gharavi
Gourmet Pantry & Cooking School
Blacksburg Fork and Cork

Vegetarian Chili

1 tablespoon olive oil
1 onion, chopped
2 garlic cloves, chopped
1 tablespoon chili powder
1 teaspoon ground cumin
1 teaspoon oregano
¼ teaspoon cinnamon
1 (10-ounce) can diced tomatoes
   with green chilies
4 cups vegetable broth
1 (15-ounce) can kernel corn
   (or equivalent fresh or frozen)

1 (15-ounce) can kidney beans,
   drained and rinsed
1 (15-ounce) can black beans,
   drained and rinsed
1 zucchini, cut into chunks
1 medium potato, cut into chunks
5 mushrooms, sliced
Splash balsamic vinegar
Splash Worcestershire sauce
Salt and Pepper to taste

In a large pot, heat oil over medium heat. Sauté onion and garlic, cooking until soft. Add chili powder, cumin, oregano and cinnamon. Cook 1 minute. Add remaining ingredients and cook until potatoes are tender. Can be served as is or over rice.

Margaret
Buckland Farm Market

White Chicken Chili

2 tablespoons olive oil
1 yellow onion large, diced
1 tablespoon garlic, minced
2 pounds cooked chicken breast,
    chopped
2 teaspoons sea salt
2 teaspoons cracked black pepper
2 tablespoons ground cumin
1 tablespoon fennel seed
1 tablespoon dried oregano

2 teaspoons chili powder
2 (15-ounce) cans white beans, rinsed
    and drained
2 (4½-ounce) cans chopped green
    chilies, undrained
1 (15½-ounce) can chicken broth
1 cup shredded Monterey Jack cheese
½ cup chopped fresh cilantro
½ cup chopped green onions

In large Dutch oven, heat oil over medium-high heat. Add onion and cook 5 minutes or until translucent. Add garlic and cook 30 seconds. Add chicken and all seasonings, stirring well. Add beans, green chilies and chicken broth. Simmer 1 hour. Serve topped with cheese, cilantro and green onion.

Chef Randall Spencer
Blue Ridge Mountain Catering
Blacksburg Fork and Cork

Fiesta Red Chicken Chili

1 pound skinless, boneless
 chicken
½ Vidalia onion, diced
½ green bell pepper, diced
½ red bell pepper, diced
¾ (12-ounce) bottle amber beer
1 (64-ounce) can tomato juice
1 (10½-ounce) can tomato soup
1 (15-ounce) can kidney beans,
 drained and rinsed

1 (15-ounce) can black beans,
 drained and rinsed
1 (15-ounce) can corn, drained and
 rinsed
1 cup salsa
1 teaspoon cracked black pepper
1 teaspoon ground red pepper
2 teaspoons cumin
⅔ cup dark brown sugar

In small skillet, cook chicken, onions and all bell peppers in shallow bath of beer over medium heat 15 minutes or until chicken is no longer pink in middle. Remove chicken and shred with a fork. Strain peppers and onions. In large pot, combine all ingredients. Bring to a boil while stirring often and reduce to simmer. Simmer 30 minutes, stirring occasionally.

Chef Randall Spencer
Blue Ridge Mountain Catering
Blacksburg Fork and Cork

Ahi Tuna Salad

1 tablespoon Canola oil
8 ounce Ahi Tuna Steak, sashimi grade
1 tablespoon white sesame seeds, toasted
4 cups mixed greens
½ cup matchstick-cut cucumber
½ cup diced tomatoes
¼ cup red bell pepper strips

Using a sauté pan, heat oil over medium heat, reserving 1 teaspoon oil. Coat Ahi steak with reserved oil, then crust both side with sesame seeds. Sear each side 30 seconds. Transfer to cutting board. Slice into thin strips. In large mixing bowl, combine mixed greens, cucumber, tomatoes and red bell pepper. Divide greens between two chilled plates and top with Ahi tuna strips.

Chef Randall Spencer
Blue Ridge Mountain Catering
Blacksburg Fork and Cork

Seared Tuna atop Greens with Virginia Goat Cheese, Bay Seasoned Pepitas and Citrus Vinaigrette

Seared Tuna:

1 (20-ounce) tuna steak, 1-inch thick
2 teaspoons salt
1 teaspoon freshly ground black pepper
½ teaspoon crushed red pepper
1 tablespoon butter
3 tablespoons olive oil

Season both sides of tuna with salt, black pepper and red pepper. Melt butter and oil in skillet over medium-high heat. Place tuna in skillet and cook 2 minutes per side for rare and 3 minutes per side for medium-rare. Remove from pan, allow to sit briefly and cut into quarter-inch slices.

Seasoned Pepitas:

1 cup pumpkin or squash seeds
1 tablespoon canola oil
1 teaspoon Chesapeake Bay seasoning mix

Scoop seeds from pumpkin or squash, rinse off pulp and pat dry. In a medium bowl, combine seeds, oil and seasoning; toss to coat. Place on baking sheet and bake at 350° for 30 to 40 minutes, turning occasionally. Seeds should turn golden but do not burn.

Citrus Vinaigrette:

½ cup freshly squeezed orange juice
¼ cup freshly squeezed lemon juice
¼ cup extra virgin olive oil
1 teaspoon Dijon mustard
½ teaspoon salt
⅛ teaspoon freshly ground black pepper

In a large jar with lid, combine all ingredients and shake until well mixed. Refrigerate until ready to use, shaking again just before serving.

Salad:

6 cups salad greens
Prepared tuna
Prepared pepitas
Prepared vinaigrette
Goat cheese

Divide greens among 4 plates, top with sliced tuna, pepitas and drizzle with vinaigrette. Place goat cheese on side of plate.

Chef Patrick Evans-Hylton
Virginia Beach

Broccoli Slaw

2 pounds fresh broccoli,
   chopped
2 to 4 red apples, chopped
1 cup raisins
1 cup pine nuts, chopped

1 cup mayonnaise
½ cup oil
2 tablespoons vinegar
4 tablespoons brown sugar

Combine all ingredients and toss well.

Sheila Matthew
Blackstone Arts & Crafts Festival

Ramen Cole Slaw

2 packages chicken or beef flavored ramen noodles
1 (16-ounce) package shredded cabbage
1 bunch green onions, thinly sliced
1 cup sunflower seeds
½ package toasted almond slivers

Crunch noodles. Mix noodles, cabbage, onions, sunflower seed and almonds.

Dressing:
½ cup oil
½ cup sugar
½ cup vinegar
2 Ramen seasoning packets

Mix all ingredients. Add to cabbage mixture just before serving.

Virginia Highlands Festival

Cornbread Salad

1 cup mayonnaise
¼ cup pickle juice
4 medium tomatoes, peeled and
  chopped
1 medium green bell pepper,
  chopped

1 medium onion
½ cup chopped sweet pickles
9 slices bacon, cooked and
  crumbled
1 box Jiffy cornbread mix

Mix mayonnaise and pickle juice; refrigerate. Combine tomatoes, bell pepper, onion, sweet pickles and bacon; set aside. Bake cornbread according to package directions; cool and crumble. In a large glass bowl, place a layer of ½ cornbread, a layer of ½ tomato mixture, and finish with ½ mayonnaise mixture; repeat. Refrigerate 2 hours before serving.

Linda Scarborough
Wise County Famous Fall Fling

Wildflower at Edith J. Carrier Arboretum

Strawberry-Banana Luscious Salad

2 small packages strawberry-banana Jell-O
2 cups boiling water
1 large package frozen strawberries, undrained
1 small can crushed pineapple, undrained
2 large ripe bananas, whipped
Pecans, optional
1 cup sour cream

Dissolve Jell-O in boiling water. Add strawberries, pineapple, bananas and nuts. Pour ½ mixture in mold or glass pan. Chill until slightly set. Pour sour cream on top and add remaining gelatin mixture. Chill until firm.

James River State Park

Lazy Day Susan

1 large can pineapple in heavy syrup
1 large can fruit cocktail, drained
1 small can Mandarin oranges, drained
1 (8-ounce) carton Cool Whip
1 box vanilla instant pudding
1 small can coconut
1 cup crushed nuts
Sugar to taste

Combine all ingredients. Serve chilled.

Margaret Staton
Virginia Southern Gospel Jubilee

Pasta Salad

8 ounces pasta, any type
½ small red onion, chopped

Choose 3 of the following vegetables:
1 medium tomato, chopped
1 small zucchini, sliced
¼ cup chopped celery
¼ cup sliced carrots
½ cup chopped broccoli
¼ cup favorite salad dressing

Prepare pasta according to package directions. Steam fresh vegetables 3 to 5 minutes. Add vegetables to pasta and stir in salad dressing.

Crossing at the Dan

Black and Blue Salad

This is an easy salad to make and very filling. The quantity of all items is up to the individual. You can use any dried or fresh fruit and any type of meat.

Mixed greens   Blue cheese
Dates, chopped   Steak, grilled
Red onion, sliced thin

Combine all ingredients and toss well.

Balsamic Vinaigrette:
1 cup balsamic vinegar   ½ teaspoon fresh garlic
½ cup olive oil   Salt and pepper to taste
¼ cup water   1 tablespoon Italian seasoning

Combine all ingredients and blend well.

Shaena Muldoon, owner
The Palisades Restaurant

Lentil Salad

1½ cups French green lentils, rinsed and picked over
3½ cups water
1 cup chopped onion
1 or 2 sprigs fresh thyme
1 bay leaf
½ teaspoon salt
Pinch ground cloves, optional

Place lentils, water, onion, thyme, bay leaf, salt and ground cloves into medium saucepan. Bring to a boil, cover and reduce heat, simmering 30 minutes (lentils should retain shape but be cooked through). Cool to lukewarm and drain any remaining liquid. Pour lentils into mixing bowl and discard herbs.

Dressing:
2 to 3 tablespoons white-wine vinegar
4 tablespoons virgin olive oil
½ teaspoon salt
¼ teaspoon freshly ground pepper
1 tablespoon Dijon-style mustard, optional
Tabasco to taste
1 large tomato, chopped into ½-inch pieces
⅓ cup finely chopped onion
2 garlic cloves, minced
2 tablespoons chopped fresh chives, for garnish

Mix vinegar, olive oil, salt, pepper, mustard and Tabasco. Add tomato, onion and garlic; combine well. Pour over warm lentils and toss gently. Sprinkle with chopped chives before serving.

Roya Gharavi
Gourmet Pantry & Cooking School
Blacksburg Fork and Cork

Quinoa & Red Rice Salad with Fruit, Walnuts & Pumpkin Seeds

2½ cups water, salted
1 cup Bhutanese Red Rice
1 cup quinoa
¼ cup olive oil, divided
1 onion, diced
Salt and freshly ground pepper
⅓ cup fresh orange juice
1½ teaspoons finely grated orange zest

1 tablespoon fresh lemon juice
1 garlic clove, minced
½ cup dried apricots or dried fruit mix, diced
½ cup chopped roasted walnuts
½ cup roasted pumpkin seeds
½ cup thinly sliced green onion
2 cups arugula

In a medium saucepan, bring salted water to a boil. Add rice, cover and simmer over medium to low heat until tender, about 25 to 30 minutes. Drain and rinse with cold water; set aside. Rinse quinoa until water runs clear. Place quinoa in saucepan with enough water to cover and bring to a boil. Reduce heat to low, cover and cook 15 minutes. Remove from heat and set aside. In a medium skillet, heat 1 tablespoon olive oil; add onion and season to taste with salt and pepper. Cook over medium heat 8 to 10 minutes or until golden brown. In a large bowl, combine orange juice, orange zest, lemon juice, garlic and remaining olive oil. Season with salt and pepper. Add quinoa, rice, onion, apricots, walnuts, pumpkin seeds and green onion; toss well. Serve with arugula.

Roya Gharavi
Gourmet Pantry & Cooking School
Blacksburg Fork and Cork

Olive Crostini

1 cup pitted black olives
1 cup green olives w/pimento
4 garlic cloves
1 cup Parmesan cheese
1 stick butter

4 teaspoons olive oil
1 cup grated Monterey Jack
 cheese
2 tablespoons fresh parsley
2 baguettes

Chop olives in food processor; set aside. Place garlic, Parmesan cheese, butter and olive oil in food processor. Blend, making a paste. Combine olives and paste in bowl. Fold in Monterey Jack cheese and parsley. Slice baguettes thinly. Spread mixture on slices. Broil 1 to 2 minutes or until bubbly.

South Hill Wine Festival

South Hill Wine Festival

September

Centennial Park • South Hill
434-447-4547
www.southhillrotary.com

Each year, the South Hill Rotary Club and Chamber of Commerce come together to sponsor the South Hill Wine Festival. "Come for the Wine...Stay for the Weekend" and enjoy an event featuring Virginia wineries, local artists, craft vendors, food from local restaurants and music throughout the day. Come early and take tours of the Model Railroad Train Museum, the Virginia S. Evans Doll Museum located in The Chamber of Commerce Depot building, the Tobacco Farm Life Museum of Virginia (located just down the street), the newly renovated Colonial Center and much more all within walking distance. This fun event raises funds for local school programs such as high school scholarships, the Dictionary Project for third graders, the Rotary International's End Polio Now Campaign and many more community interests. Tickets are $20 in advance and $25 at the gate and include one wine glass and tasting. For more information contact 434-447-4547 or visit www.southhillrotaryclub.org or www.southhillchamber.com. If you live nearby, watch the local papers and listen to local radio for additional details. Tickets are available for purchase online at www.southhillrotary.com and at the South Hill Chamber of Commerce.

Miss Eloise's Afternoon Tea Bread

The Shop at The Hunter House Victorian Museum offers Miss Eloise's Afternoon Tea, a lovely jasmine flavored black tea.

2 cups flour
2 teaspoons baking powder
½ teaspoon salt
½ teaspoon cinnamon
2 large eggs, slightly beaten
1 cup sugar
¼ cup vegetable oil
1 cup strongly brewed Jasmine tea, at room temperature
3 tablespoons honey
1 tablespoon fresh lemon juice

Preheat oven to 375°. Lightly coat 9x5-inch loaf pan with nonstick cooking spray. In large bowl, sift together flour, baking powder, salt and cinnamon. In another large bowl, whisk together eggs, sugar, oil and tea until well mixed. Whisking slowly, add dry mix to liquid mix. Mix just until moistened. Spoon batter into loaf pan and bake 50 minutes or until golden brown. While bread is baking combine honey and lemon juice in small bowl. When bread is done and still warm, brush top with honey glaze. Cool bread 10 minutes in baking pan. Remove to wire rack to cool completely.

Hunter House Victorian Museum

Spoon Bread

½ cup cornmeal
½ teaspoon salt
1 cup boiling water
2 tablespoons butter, melted
2 eggs, beaten
1½ cups milk

Preheat oven to 400°. Combine cornmeal and salt. Pour water over mixture. Stir well and cool. Add butter, eggs and milk; blend well. Pour into hot greased pan. Bake 40 minutes or until firm.

Stratford Hall

San Domingo Corncakes

1 egg
1 cup buttermilk
1 tablespoon vegetable oil
1 cup golden meal flour
1 tablespoon sugar

1 teaspoon baking powder
1 teaspoon baking soda
½ teaspoon salt
½ cup whole-kernel corn

Blend egg, buttermilk and oil. Add dry ingredients. When mixed well, add corn. Pour in small circles onto hot griddle (same method as making pancakes). Serve with syrup, powdered sugar or cinnamon.

Lola Galvan, Baldemar Galvan and Lillian Casper
San Domingo Ranch
Representatives for Native Americans, International Children's Festival

Old Fashioned Corn Pancakes

2 cups raw sweet corn scraped,
   not cut, from the cob
1 egg, beaten
⅔ cup flour

½ cup milk
1 teaspoon baking powder
½ teaspoon salt
¼ teaspoon ground black pepper

Crush corn kernels to release corn 'cream'. Combine all ingredients, adjusting milk and flour for desired consistency. Cook on greased hot cast iron griddle. Makes 12 pancakes.

"Corn Acoustics!" Corn Maze
Mountain Meadow Farm

Rockingham County Fair

Slapjacks

Served on the farm site.

1 cup milk	4 eggs
2 cups flour	4 tablespoons cornmeal

Combine all ingredients. (Batter should be same consistency as pancake batter.) Cook on buttered griddle over medium heat. Flip when bubbles show on top. Serve warm with butter, salt or honey.

Claude Moore Colonial Farm

Norwegian Vafler (Waffles)

The vafler in Norway are served as dessert or as a heart-shaped treat. They are much sweeter and softer than American waffles and are almost always homemade.

6 eggs	Pinch salt
½ cup sugar	1 cup sour cream
1 teaspoon ground cardamom	½ cup melted butter
1½ cups flour	3 tablespoons butter for cooking
1 teaspoon baking powder	

Mix eggs, sugar and cardamom together in large bowl. Add flour, baking powder and salt; mix well. Add sour cream and melted butter. Blend until smooth. Let batter sit 20 minutes. Heat waffle iron and brush surface with butter. Pour ¼ cup batter in iron and cook until golden brown. Serve warm.

June Cooper
Representative for Norway, International Children's Festival

Cherry Stuffed French Toast

Delicious served with Ole' Virginia Pancake Syrup from the The Country Canner.

8 eggs
¼ cup milk
1 teaspoon vanilla extract
½ teaspoon cinnamon
¼ teaspoon nutmeg
¼ teaspoon salt
12 slices French bread (½-inch thick)

1 (8-ounce) package cream cheese,
  softened
1 (16-ounce) jar Cherry Pie Filling from
  The Country Canner
2 tablespoons butter
Powdered sugar

In a large mixing bowl, beat together eggs, milk, vanilla, cinnamon, nutmeg and salt; set aside. Spread cream cheese on each slice bread. Spread pie filling over 6 bread slices. Cover each slice with remaining bread slices, cream cheese side down. Dip into egg mixture. In skillet, cook sandwiches in hot butter over medium heat 2 to 3 minutes on each side or until golden brown. Make sure each is cooked through the middle. Cut into halves or quarters and sprinkle with powdered sugar.

The Country Canner

Overnight French Toast

¼ cup butter, softened
12 French bread slices, ¾-inch
   thick
6 eggs
1½ cups milk

¼ cup sugar
2 tablespoons maple syrup
1 teaspoon vanilla extract
Cinnamon to taste

Spread butter in bottom of large glass baking dish. Arrange bread slices in dish. In large bowl combine eggs, milk, sugar, syrup, and vanilla; beat well. Pour mixture over bread. Turn bread slices to coat. Cover with plastic and refrigerate overnight. Before baking, sprinkle with cinnamon. Bake at 400° for 15 minutes. Turn bread and cook additional 15 minutes. Delicious served with butter, powdered sugar and maple syrup.

Judy and Clyde Beachy
Edinburg Mill

Edinburg Mill

214 South Main Street • Edinburg
540-984-8400

The Edinburg Mill has been a centerpiece of Edinburg society since it was constructed by Major George Grandstaff in 1848. It is one of only a few mills that survived the Civil War; it continued to serve as a working mill until 1979 when it was converted into a restaurant that operated until 1998. The Town of Edinburg and the Edinburg Heritage Foundation purchased the Mill in 2000.

The 20,000-square foot building is a designated Virginia Historic Landmark and on the National Register of Historic Places. It now houses a visitor center, museum, retail shops and restaurant. The museum tells the history of the building and Town along with the Valley Pike and area transportation and features "The Burning," a film based on John Heatwole's book about the Civil War.

Baked French Toast

1 loaf white bread, cubed, divided
1 (8-ounce) package cream cheese, cubed
8 to 12 eggs, depending on size
½ cup maple syrup
1 cup milk

Place ½ bread cubes in 11x13-inch pan. Layer cream cheese on top of bread. Cover with remaining bread cubes. Beat eggs, maple syrup and milk together. Pour mixture over bread. Cover and refrigerate overnight. Bake at 350° for 45 minutes or until light golden brown.

Mary Boerner
Daffodil Festival

Edinburg Ole Time Festival

Edinburg Ole Time Festival is a 3-day annual event that begins the third Friday of September. Started in 1980 around the Edinburg Mill, it is a town-wide celebration with a parade, arts, crafts, food, entertainment, antique cars and tractors and so much more.

www.edinburgoletimefestival.org

Fry Bread

This is a tasty, fun recipe for camping trips.

2 cups flour
1½ tablespoons powdered milk
½ teaspoon salt

3 teaspoons baking powder
¾ cup warm water
½ tablespoon shortening

Mix dry ingredients. Add warm water gradually. Knead until dough is soft, but not sticky. Shape into 2-inch balls. Flatten into circles and make hole in center. Melt shortening in skillet over medium-high heat and fry dough until lightly browned. Drain on paper towels.

Matt Stickley
Grand Caverns

Banana Bread

1 stick butter, softened
2 eggs
1⅔ cups sugar
1 teaspoon vanilla
4 small ripe bananas, mashed

1 teaspoon lemon juice
1 cup sour cream
2¼ cups flour
2¾ teaspoons baking powder
1 teaspoon baking soda

Preheat oven to 325°. Combine butter, eggs, sugar and vanilla. In a separate bowl, mix together bananas, lemon juice, and sour cream. Combine 2 mixtures. Add flour, baking powder and baking soda. Pour into 2 greased and floured loaf pans. Bake 40 to 50 minutes.

Linda Phillips
General's Ridge Vineyard

Boston Beer Muffins

½ cup rye flour
½ cup whole wheat flour
½ cup yellow cornmeal
1½ teaspoons baking soda
¾ teaspoon salt
1 cup buttermilk

⅓ cup dark brown sugar
⅓ cup molasses
⅓ cup favorite dark beer
1 egg
1 cup raisins

Preheat oven 400°. Grease 12 muffin cups or line with paper baking cups. Combine rye flour, wheat flour, cornmeal, baking soda and salt in large bowl. In a separate bowl, combine buttermilk, brown sugar, molasses, beer and egg. Add to flour mixture along with raisins; stir until combined. Fill prepared muffin cups. Bake 15 minutes or until toothpick inserted into center comes out clean. Delicious served with cream cheese.

Chef Randall Spencer
Blue Ridge Mountain Catering
Blacksburg Fork and Cork

Blacksburg Fork and Cork

Quick Cheddar Bread

3⅓ cups biscuit mix
2½ cups grated sharp Cheddar Cheese
2 eggs, slightly beaten
1¼ cups milk

Combine biscuit mix with cheese. In separate bowl, combine eggs and milk. Stir into cheese mixture, mixing just enough to moisten. Bake in greased and floured 9x5-inch loaf pan at 350° for 55 minutes.

Barbara Barger
Virginia Southern Gospel Jubilee

Virginia Southern Gospel Jubilee

July

**Glen Maury Park • 540-261-7321
Buena Vista
www.VaSouthernGospelJubilee.com
Pastor Larry Clark • 540-261-2556**

One of the most exciting and well attended annual events is The Virginia Southern Gospel Jubilee. Hundreds of people attend this free event sponsored by The Pentecostal Outreach Church in Buena Vista. Professional Southern gospel singing groups from around the country, along with some local talent, perform each evening. There is food, free parking, camping and singing, rain or shine! Denominations of all types gather under the pavilion to worship in song and music.

Z' Bread

3 eggs
2 cups sugar
1 cup oil
1 teaspoon vanilla
2 cups grated zucchini
2 cups flour
1 teaspoon salt

1 teaspoon cinnamon
½ teaspoon baking soda
½ teaspoon baking
  powder
½ teaspoon ground cloves
½ teaspoon nutmeg
1 cup chopped nuts

Preheat oven to 350°. Grease and flour 2 loaf pans or 1 Bundt pan. Beat eggs until creamy. Add sugar, oil and vanilla; mix until smooth. Add zucchini and continue mixing. Add remaining ingredients, stir thoroughly and pour into pans. Bake 1 hour.

Sandy Yun
Wise County Famous Fall Fling

Angel Biscuits

1 package yeast
2 tablespoons lukewarm water
5 cups flour
1 teaspoon baking soda
3 teaspoons baking powder
4 teaspoons sugar
1 teaspoon salt
1 cup shortening
2 cups buttermilk

Dissolve yeast in lukewarm water. Sift together flour, baking soda, baking powder, sugar and salt. Cut in shortening. Add buttermilk and yeast mixture. Stir until flour is dissolved. Knead on floured board 1 to 2 minutes. Roll dough to ½-inch thick. Cut with biscuit cutter. Bake at 400° for 45 to 50 minutes or until center is done.

James River State Park

Tomato Gravy

1 quart tomato juice, divided
3 tablespoons plain flour
¾ cup sugar

2 teaspoons salt
½ stick butter

Put juice in a 2-quart stew pan, reserving 1 cup. Heat to almost boiling. Mix flour and sugar with reserved tomato juice until smooth. Gradually add to pan while stirring. Cook 2 minutes. Add salt and butter and stir until smooth. Serve over hot biscuits with a side of country ham.

Madeline Grant, Montebello
Montebello Camping & Fishing Resort

Huckleberry Jam

First appeared in The Southern Planter *magazine, June 1937.*

To prepare fruit:

1½ quarts fully ripe berries   Juice from 1 lemon
Zest from ½ lemon

Crush berries. Add zest and juice; mix well.

Jam:

4½ cups prepared fruit   1 bottle fruit pectin
7 cups sugar

Combine prepared fruit and sugar in large pot; mix well. Bring to rolling boil over high heat, stirring constantly. Boil hard 2 minutes. Remove from heat and stir in fruit pectin. Skim; pour quickly into sterilized glass jars.

Morven Park

Morven Park

Open Year Round
703-777-2414 • www.MorvenPark.org

A National Register Historic Property, Morven Park was once the home of Virginia Governor Westmoreland Davis. Through programs offered at its three museums, sports and equestrian complex, and 1,200 acres of open space, Morven Park continues to reflect the ideals advanced by Governor Davis – civic responsibility, agricultural sustainability, and improvement of life for rural Virginians. Morven Park is a non-profit organization, operated by the Westmoreland Davis Memorial Foundation. More than 75,000 people visit each year, participating in the captivating programming and touring the Greek Revival mansion, beautiful scenery, historic gardens, sports fields, Civil War encampment site, and hiking trails. Public events occur throughout the year, including Civil War reenactments, equestrian competitions, festivals and hands-on learning programs. Grounds are open 8am to dusk every day except Thanksgiving, Christmas, and New Year's Day. Tours of the Governor's manor are Monday, Thursday, Friday, Saturday and Sunday, from 11am to 5pm, April through October. November through March the hours change to noon to 4pm.

Elderberry Jelly

First appeared in The Southern Planter *magazine, June 1937.*

Juice:

4 pounds fully ripe elderberries   **4 medium lemons**

Remove larger stems from berries; place in kettle and crush. Heat gently until juice starts to flow. Simmer, covered, 15 minutes. Place fruit in jelly cloth or bag and squeeze juice into clean container. Squeeze and strain juice from lemons, adding to berry juice.

Jelly:

3 cups berry juice   **7½ cups sugar**
½ cup lemon juice (additional)   **1 bottle fruit pectin**

Combine berry juice, lemon juice and sugar in large saucepan. Bring to boil over high heat and add fruit pectin, stirring constantly. Bring to full rolling boil and boil hard ½ minute. Remove from heat, skim and pour quickly. Store immediately in sterilized glass jars.

Morven Park

Morven Park

Lavender Butter Sauce

¾ cup sugar
⅓ cup butter
3 tablespoons water
1 teaspoon culinary lavender buds

In saucepan, combine sugar, butter and water; bring to boil. Remove from heat. Add lavender buds and sit 15 minutes (strain lavender if desired). Pour sauce over cake or muffins.

White Oak Lavender Farm

White Oak Lavender Farm

Pepper Butter

22 hot peppers	6 cups sugar
22 sweet peppers	1 tablespoon salt
1 pint yellow mustard	1 cup flour
1 quart vinegar	1½ cups water

Grind peppers in food processor and put into pot. Add mustard, vinegar, sugar and salt. Bring to boil. In a separate bowl, make paste with flour and water. Add to boiling mixture and cook 5 minutes, stirring constantly. Put into sterilized jars and seal.

Lettie Stickley
Grand Caverns

Vegetables & Other Side Dishes

French-Style Green Bean Casserole

3 cans French-style green beans, drained
¼ cup milk
3 tablespoons flour
2 tablespoons butter
1 cup grated Swiss cheese
2 tablespoons dried onion
1 teaspoon sugar
1 can cream of shrimp soup
1 cup sour cream
Salt and pepper to taste
1 cup crushed cornflakes

Preheat oven to 350°. Pour green beans in casserole dish; set aside. In saucepan, combine milk, flour, butter, cheese, onion, sugar, soup, sour cream, salt and pepper. Heat over medium-low heat, stirring constantly. Pour over green beans. Sprinkle cornflakes over top. Cook 45 minutes.

DelFosse Vineyards and Winery

Aunt Freda's Green Beans

2 quarts fresh green beans
1 slice onion, diced thin
½ cup olive oil
4 chicken bullion cubes

Place green beans in large pot and cover with water. Boil water halfway down and add remaining ingredients. Continuing boiling down until very little water remains. Green beans should be tender and full of flavor.

Tressia Boyd
Richlands Fall Festival

Edamame

10 cups salted water
1 (16-ounce) bag frozen edamame
½ teaspoon Chinese red peppercorn
½ teaspoon salt

½ teaspoon black pepper
2 star anise
1 tablespoon sesame oil

Bring water to boil. Place edamame into water and boil 3 to 4 minutes. In a separate bowl, combine peppercorns, salt, black pepper, star anise and 1 tablespoon boiling water. Drain edamame. Pour into bowl, add sesame oil; toss well. May be eaten hot or cold.

Karen Chen
Representative for Taiwan R.O.C., International Children's Festival

Virginia Baked Beans

½ cup chopped onion
⅓ cup white sugar
⅓ cup brown sugar
¼ cup barbeque sauce
¼ cup ketchup
2 tablespoons mustard
2 tablespoons molasses
½ teaspoon salt

½ teaspoon chili powder
½ teaspoon pepper
10 slices cooked bacon, cut into ½-inch
  pieces
1 (16-ounce) can red beans
1 (16-ounce) can pork and beans
1 (16-ounce) can butter beans

Combine all ingredients and pour into 9x13-inch baking dish. Bake at 350°, uncovered, for 1¼ hours.

Janice Kiehl
The Virginia Lovers' Gourd Society
Virginia Gourd Festival

Virginia Gourd Festival

November

Richards Fruit Market
Middletown
Hosted by the Virginia Lovers' Gourd Society
www.virginialoversgourdsociety.org

The Virginia Lovers' Gourd Society is the Delta chapter of the American Gourd Society, a national organization devoted to the inedible part of the squash family. The VLGS is a collection of gourd enthusiasts who enjoy growing gourds and then using the dehydrated fruits of the vine to make art and crafts.

The Virginia Gourd Festival is their annual public event involving classes, demonstrations, and an auction along with a marketplace for buying gourd art for the collector and gourd supplies for the crafter. It is a real celebration of fun and gourd joy!

Historically, hard-shelled gourds have been used as grain and milk carriers, powder horns and water dippers in many ancient cultures. Although bottleneck gourds are commonly used as birdhouses, other gourd shapes are used to make bowls, jars, ornaments, and whatever else a clever person can invent—it's all in the imagination. Check out the Virginia Gourd Festival and you too can become a gourdhead!

Pinto Beans

2 tablespoons olive oil
1 onion, diced
3 garlic cloves, sliced
2 banana peppers, sliced
1 carrot, diced
2 tablespoons tomato paste
2 tomatoes, diced

1 (24-ounce) can pinto beans
1 teaspoon salt
1 teaspoon pepper
1 teaspoon crushed pepper flakes
1 cup water
½ cup finely chopped parsley

Heat oil in large pot over medium heat. Sauté onion, garlic, banana pepper and carrots 5 to 10 minutes. Add tomato paste and stir 2 minutes. Add tomatoes and simmer 5 minutes. Add pinto beans, salt, pepper, pepper flakes and water. Simmer 20 to 25 minutes. Stir in parsley and turn off. Serve with fresh bread or rice. Best when served at room temperature.

Dee King
Representative for Turkey, International Children's Festival

State Arboretum of Virginia

Blandy Experimental Farm
540-837-1758
www.Blandy.virginia.edu

The Virginia Lovers' Gourd Society proudly participates in the Blandy Community Garden at the State Arboretum of Virginia. Blandy's Community Garden was established Spring 2008 as a way for local families and groups to grow vegetables for their own use and for donation. In exchange for garden space, gardeners agree to donate a portion of what they grow to area food banks, soup kitchens, and families in need. The fenced garden includes 25 plots, 75 feet of raised beds, and an arbor.

The arbor is the space where the VLGS grows gourds as an educational outreach program. All throughout the season, gardeners and their children learn about gourds and the long history of gourd use as garden scoops, water sprinklers, and, of course, birdhouses! Gourds grown in the arbor are used in the chapter's Spring Gourd Fling when Arboretum friends and families are invited to a free hands-on workshop.

Texas Caviar

¾ cup cider vinegar
½ cup light salad oil
1 cup sugar
Salt and pepper to taste
1 can black beans
1 can black-eyed peas
1 can kidney beans

1 can pinto beans
1 can shoepeg corn
1 red bell pepper, seeded and
    chopped
1 green bell pepper, seeded and
    chopped
½ Vidalia onion, chopped

In saucepan, combine vinegar, oil, sugar, salt and pepper; bring to a boil, stirring occasionally. Remove from heat and cool completely. Drain and rinse all beans and corn. In large bowl, combine vinegar mixture, beans, corn, peppers and onion; toss well. Refrigerate overnight. Remove oil on top before serving.

Edinburg Mill

Edinburg Mill, Old Town Festival

Beets with Yogurt

2 pounds beets
2 garlic cloves, crushed
2 cups strained yogurt
2 tablespoons lemon juice
6 tablespoons olive oil
Salt
Handful chopped mint or
    flat-leaf parsley

Cut stems and leaves about ¾-inch above beets. Place beets in a large pot and cover with salted water; bring to a boil. Cook until tender. Small beets will take around 30 minutes, larger beets up to an hour. Allow beets to cool and cut into ½-inch thick rounds or half moon slices. In a bowl, mix crushed garlic into yogurt and mix well. Spread yogurt mixture onto serving plate and arrange beet slices on top. In a separate bowl, mix lemon juice, olive oil and salt. Stir in chopped mint or parsley. Spoon over beet slices.

Roya Gharavi
Gourmet Pantry & Cooking School
Blacksburg Fork and Cork

Harvard Beets

1 can sliced beets
¾ cup sugar
¼ teaspoon salt
1½ tablespoons cornstarch
¼ cup vinegar
1 tablespoon butter

Drain beets and reserve juice; set beets aside. In a saucepan, combine sugar, salt, cornstarch, vinegar and reserved beet juice until clear and thick, stirring constantly. Add beets and butter. Cook 20 minutes. Serve warm.

Abigail Kime
B(l) Country Store

Broccoli Casserole

1 head fresh broccoli, cut into pieces
1 (10½-ounce) can cream of
　　mushroom soup
⅔ cup grated Cheddar cheese

2 tablespoons finely chopped onion
2 eggs, beaten
1 cup mayonnaise
2 cups Ritz cracker crumbs

Cook broccoli until tender. Mix soup, cheese, onion, eggs and mayonnaise together. Gently stir in broccoli. Pour into greased glass dish. Top with cracker crumbs. Bake at 350° for 30 to 40 minutes.

Rita Longworth
Wise County Famous Fall Fling

Wise County Famous Fall Fling
October

Courthouse Mall • Wise
276-328-6842
www.wisefallfling.com

Nestled in the heart of Appalachia and on the Crooked Road, along Virginia's Heritage Music Trail, is Wise, population 3,200. Both historic and a community on the move, Wise is home to the County's historic courthouse, historic homes and businesses, and the University of Virginia's College

at Wise, a top liberal arts school. The downtown community offers shopping and dining options ranging from quaint to contemporary.

Each fall, the second weekend in October, downtown Wise comes alive for the Wise Fall Fling, a free festival held while fall color in the mountains is at its peak. About 150 vendors selling crafts, food, jewelry and more offer their wares alongside craft demonstrators, all while live traditional music ranging from banjos to bagpipes is played. The event also features essay, photo and art contests, a chili cook-off and a 5K race.

Broccoli Casserole

2 (10-ounce) packages frozen chopped broccoli
1 cup mayonnaise
1 cup grated sharp Cheddar cheese
1 can cream of mushroom soup
2 eggs, beaten
1 sleeve Ritz crackers

Boil broccoli in salted water until tender; drain. Add mayonnaise, cheese, soup and eggs; mix well. Pour into 2-quart greased casserole dish. Cover with crumbled Ritz crackers. Bake at 350° for 45 minutes.

Deborah B. Borum
Blackstone Arts & Crafts Festival

Bernard's Butternut Squash Casserole

3 butternut squash, cooked,
  hulled (chopped)
¾ cup sugar
1½ teaspoons vanilla extract

3 eggs
2 tablespoons cornstarch
½ stick melted butter
Grated nutmeg to taste

Combine squash, sugar, vanilla, eggs and cornstarch. Pour into casserole dish and top with butter. Sprinkle with nutmeg. Bake at 300° for 45 minutes.

Reverend Bernard LeSuer
Culpeper Air Fest

Butternut Squash Apple Cranberry Bake

1 large butternut squash, peeled and cut into 1-inch cubes
2 large tart cooking apples, peeled and cut into ½-inch thick slices
½ cup fresh or frozen cranberries (may substitute with craisins)
½ cup brown sugar
1 tablespoon flour
1 teaspoon salt
½ teaspoon ground mace (may substitute ground nutmeg)
¼ cup butter

Preheat oven to 350°. Line squash in bottom of ungreased 7x11-inch baking dish. Place apples on top, followed by cranberries. In separate bowl, combine sugar, flour, salt and mace; sprinkle on top. Dot with butter. Bake 50 to 60 minutes.

Donna Parris
River District Festival

Coastal Grill's Signature Acorn Squash

4 acorn squash
Butter to taste
4 tablespoons brown sugar, divided

Preheat oven to 400°. Split acorn squash in half from stem to tip. With spoon, scoop out all seeds. On a sheet pan or pie tin, place squash hollowed side down and add ½-inch water. Bake 35 to 40 minutes, or until you can prick the skin with a knife. (Be careful not to punch too large a hole in squash, it will not hold butter.) Invert squash and add butter and 1 tablespoon brown sugar to each.

Chef Jerry Bryan
Coastal Grill

Fresh Pumpkin

Conversion of fresh pumpkin for recipes calling for canned pumpkin.

Cooking Fresh Pumpkin:

Wash pumpkin with clean water and cut into half or quarters, depending on size. Clean out seeds. Pumpkin can be microwaved on high or baked in an oven at 400°. Cook until tender, watching carefully.

Cool to room temperature. Remove meat from skin. Run meat through food processor or use potato masher. Substitute in any recipe calling for canned pumpkin.

Leftover pumpkin can be frozen and will keep frozen for about 1 year.

Crossing at the Dan

Savory Sweet Potatoes

3 pounds sweet potatoes
Olive oil for coating
1 package French onion soup mix

Preheat oven to 400°. Peel and cube sweet potatoes. Place in large bowl and coat with olive oil; toss well. Add onion soup mix and stir, coating well. Spread on cookie sheet and bake 20 to 25 minutes or until potato cubes are tender.

Heather Chaney
South Hill Rotary Club
South Hill Wine Festival

Old Fashioned Stuffed Eggplant

2 medium eggplants, sliced
  lengthwise
1 (8-ounce) can tomato sauce, divided
1 pound ground beef or pork (may
  use half/half)
1¼ teaspoons salt

½ teaspoon black pepper
½ cup chopped onion
½ cup chopped bell pepper
1 egg, lightly beaten
½ cup quick cooking oats

Preheat oven to 375°. Hull out eggplants to ¼-inch of skin. Set skins aside and chop hulled eggplant. Combine chopped eggplant with ½ can tomato sauce (reserve remaining ½ can for topping). Mix in remaining ingredients and shape into 4 loaves. Place each loaf into an eggplant shell.

Topping:

2 tablespoons brown sugar

1 tablespoon prepared mustard

Combine remaining ½ can tomato sauce with brown sugar and mustard; mix well. Spread on loaves. Bake 1 hour or until done.

Crossing at the Dan

Crossing at the Dan

Danville
434-797-8961 • www.playdanvilleva.com

The Crossing at the Dan is located in historic downtown Danville. The Crossing began as a hub Southern Railroad, with rail houses, freight stations and rail yard. Today, the Crossing stands as a top-notch entertainment complex. Each facility hosts various special events and programs throughout the year, and is also available for private rentals. The facilities include the Pepsi Building, Community Market and Carrington Pavilion. The Danville Farmers' Market, also located at the Crossing, offers over 50 vendors selling produce, plants and flowers, baked goods, meats and unique gifts.

Cabbage Casserole

1 stick butter
½ cup mayonnaise
1 cup milk
1½ cup cornflake crumbs, divided
4 cups grated cabbage
1 cup shredded sharp Cheddar cheese

Preheat oven to 325°. In saucepan, combine butter, mayonnaise and milk over medium-low heat; reduce to simmer. Line 9x13-inch baking dish with 1 cup cornflake crumbs. Spread cabbage over crumbs, sprinkle cheese over cabbage, and pour warm butter mixture on top. Sprinkle with remaining cornflake crumbs. Bake 45 minutes.

In fond memory of Winnie "Pooh" Saulley
Grand Caverns

Grilled Asparagus

16 to 20 thin asparagus
½ cup olive oil
Salt to taste
Freshly ground black pepper to taste

Trim and wash asparagus; set aside. In a small bowl, whisk together olive oil, salt and pepper. Blanch asparagus in boiling water 1 minute. Remove and place in cold water bath. Remove and pat dry. Place on grill 4 to 8 minutes, depending on size. Brush with olive oil mixture and turn 2 or 3 times. Serve warm or at room temperature.

Sandy Pottinger
Crossing at the Dan

Potatoes Casserole

2 (10¾-ounce) cans cream of chicken soup
2 cups milk
¾ (30-ounce) package Ore-Ida frozen shredded hash browns, thawed
¼ cup chopped onions
Salt and pepper to taste
2 cups shredded sharp Cheddar cheese, divided
1 (16-ounce) carton sour cream

Preheat oven to 350°. Mix soup and milk and heat in microwave as directed on cans. In a separate bowl, combine hash browns, onions, salt and pepper. Add 1½ cups cheese and sour cream. Pour mixture into 9x13-inch pan; top with soup mixture and sprinkle with remaining cheese. Bake 50 minutes.

Faye Rakes
Hillsville Downtown Celebration Series

Hillsville Downtown Celebration Series

May, June, July, August and September

Jailhouse Square
410 North Main Street
Hillsville
276-728-2128
www.townofhillsville.com

Every summer, the town of Hillsville welcomes classic cars, music and food to its historic downtown district. Once a month, throughout the summer, locals and visitors alike pull up chairs on the lawn and enjoy a day of music and fun. Admission is always free, and children's

activities ensure a family-friendly atmosphere. So grab a chair, put on some flip-flops and come enjoy Hillsville's beach concert series. Call for band listings and schedules.

Smashed Potatoes

3 pounds potatoes washed,
    baked or microwaved
    until done
1 garlic clove, crushed
⅛ onion, chopped
½ cup shredded Cheddar
    cheese
Milk
Salt
Pepper

Peel and smash cooked potatoes and place in 1-quart dish. Add garlic, onion and Cheddar cheese. Add milk until creamy. Salt and pepper to taste. Bake at 325° for 25 minutes.

James River State Park

David's Fried Potatoes

8 red potatoes
½ teaspoon sea salt
1½ tablespoons extra virgin olive oil
Sea Salt and fresh cracked black peppercorn to taste
2 sprigs fresh rosemary leaves, chopped
Parsley

Rinse and cut potatoes into ½-inch quarter chunks. Place in large pot and fill with cold water until covered. Add sea salt. Boil until tender. Drain and rinse with cold water. Heat electric skillet to 400°. Coat skillet with olive oil and add potatoes. Season with sea salt and cracked pepper. Fry potatoes until they begin to brown. Add rosemary. Continue cooking and turning potatoes until crispy. Garnish with parsley and serve warm.

Bay View Inn Bed & Breakfast

Potato Curry

3 tablespoons oil
½ teaspoon mustard seeds
1 teaspoon Channa Dhal
1 teaspoon Urad Dhal
2 medium onions, finely chopped
4 green chilies, finely chopped
1-inch ginger, finely chopped
2 sprigs curry leaves, finely chopped

½ teaspoon red chili powder
½ teaspoon turmeric powder
1 pound potatoes, boiled, peeled,
    and cubed
Salt to taste
Handful coriander leaves, finely
    chopped

Heat oil over medium-high heat. Season with mustard seeds, Channa Dhal and Urad Dhal. Add onions, green chilies, ginger, curry leaves, chili powder and turmeric powder. Sauté until onions brown. Add potatoes and salt; mix thoroughly. Add coriander and cook until potatoes are tender. Delicious wrapped inside Dosa.

Courtesy of 'Rich Recipes'
Festival of India

Easy, Easy Potato Casserole

1 (2-pound) bag frozen hash brown potatoes
1 stick melted butter
1 cup sour cream
1 cup diced onions
1 cup shredded cheese
1 can cream of mushroom soup

Combine all ingredients and place in 9x13-inch casserole dish.

Topping:
1 cup cornflakes
1 stick butter, softened

Combine ingredients and mix thoroughly. Spread over casserole.
Bake at 325° for 1½ hours.

Doris Clore and Thelma Bradshaw
Culpeper Air Fest

Rainy Day Potato Casserole

1 (32-ounce) bag frozen cubed
   hash brown
1 medium onion, chopped
1 can cream of potato soup
1 can cream of celery soup
1 (8-ounce) carton sour cream

½ teaspoon salt
½ green bell pepper, chopped
⅛ teaspoon black pepper
6 ounces Monterey Jack cheese,
   grated

Preheat oven to 325°. Combine all ingredients except cheese. Stir
well and place in greased casserole dish. Bake 1 hour and 15 minutes. Sprinkle cheese on top and cook additional 15 minutes.

Paula Sims
Culpeper Air Fest

Corn Pudding

1 bag frozen corn
5 eggs, beaten
1 teaspoon vanilla
1 teaspoon salt
1 cup sugar
1 large can evaporated milk

Mix above ingredients; pour into greased casserole dish. Bake at 350° for 30 to 45 minutes until brown.

Bettie Musso
General's Ridge Vineyard

General's Ridge Vineyard

1618 Weldons Drive • Hague
804-223-2GRV (2478)
Tasting Room: 804-472-3172
www.generalsridgevineyard.com

Nestled in the quaint countryside of Virginia's historic Westmoreland County, located in the heart of the Northern Neck, is General's Ridge Vineyard.

Owners Richard L. (Rick) Phillips, Major General USMC (Ret) and wife, Linda, are there to give visitors a warm and gracious welcome to the 100-acre plantation. Take a step back in time and stay in the plantation's Manor House which has graced the property for 150 years or stay in the modern Vineyard Views Cottage.

The Manor House, Vineyard Views, The Carriage House and the newly constructed Vines Room and Somewhere in Time tasting rooms of General's Ridge Vineyard offer lodging and elegant facilities for special events.

Corn Casserole

1 box Jiffy Corn Muffin Mix
1 can cream-style corn
½ cup oil
1 (8-ounce) carton sour cream
½ teaspoon salt
3 eggs, separated

Preheat oven to 350°. Combine muffin mix, corn, oil, sour cream, salt and egg yolks. Beat egg whites. Slowly fold into mixture. Bake in greased casserole dish 45 minutes.

Thelma Conner
Culpeper Air Fest

Parmesan Corn

¼ cup grated Parmesan cheese
½ teaspoon Italian herb seasoning
¼ cup melted butter
¼ cup sugar, optional
4 to 5 ears sweet corn, husked

Combine Parmesan cheese, herb seasoning and melted butter; set aside. Fill a large pot with water and add sugar, if desired. Drop in corn and bring to a boil. Boil 7 to 8 minutes. Remove from water and let cool. Brush with butter mixture.

Crossing at the Dan

Fried Green Tomatoes

James River State Park's Stamp of Approval.

1 large egg, lightly beaten
½ cup buttermilk
½ cup flour, divided
½ cup cornmeal
1 teaspoon salt

½ teaspoon pepper
3 medium-size green tomatoes,
　cut into ⅓-inch slices
Vegetable oil
Salt to taste

Combine egg and buttermilk; set aside. In separate bowl, combine ¼ cup flour, cornmeal, salt and pepper. Dredge tomato slices in remaining flour and dip in egg mixture. Dredge again in cornmeal mixture. For thicker breading, repeat. Pour oil ½-inch deep in large cast-iron skillet and heat to 375°. Drop tomatoes into hot oil and cook 2 minutes on each side or until golden. Drain on paper towels. Sprinkle with salt to taste.

James River State Park

James River State Park

Stuffed Tomatoes

4 large tomatoes
1 cup corn
1 tablespoon minced onion
1 tablespoon minced parsley

¾ cup breadcrumbs, divided
Salt and pepper to taste
2 tablespoons butter

Cut tops off tomatoes; scoop out seeds and pulp, reserving 1 tablespoon pulp. Mix corn, onion, parsley, ½ cup breadcrumbs, salt, pepper and reserved pulp. Spoon mixture into tomatoes. Top each tomato with remaining breadcrumbs and ½ tablespoon butter. Bake at 350° for 20 minutes. Watch carefully, tomatoes should be baked but not mushy.

Norfolk Botanical Garden

Norfolk Botanical Garden

6700 Azalea Garden Road • Norfolk
757-441-5830
www.norfolkbotanicalgarden.org

Joann Gariety Shipley

Norfolk Botanical Garden began in 1938 and today represents an oasis of more than 40 theme gardens encompassing 155 beautiful acres. From stunning plant collections to WOW—World of Wonders: A Children's Adventure Garden, this diverse natural beauty can be explored by tram, boat, or walking tours. The Garden is accredited by the American Association of Museums, is recognized as a Virginia Historic Landmark, listed on the National Register of Historic Places, and is managed by the Norfolk Botanical Garden Society in cooperation with the City of Norfolk. The Garden is an ideal location for weddings and special celebrations. Norfolk Botanical Garden is dedicated to enriching life by promoting the enjoyment of plants and the environment through beautiful gardens and education programs. For more information, visit www. norfolkbotanicalgarden.org.

Tomato Pie

1 (10-count) package Pillsbury biscuits
4 large tomatoes, sliced and seeded
1 teaspoon basil
Salt and pepper to taste
¼ cup chopped green onion
1 cup mayonnaise
1 cup grated Monterey Jack cheese

Preheat oven to 425°. Line bottom of 10-inch pie pan with biscuits, pressing together to make crust. Layer tomato slices over crust. Sprinkle with basil, salt, pepper and green onions. Combine mayonnaise and cheese. Spread over top. Bake 12 to 15 minutes. Cool and cut into wedges.

Linda Scarborough
Wise County Famous Fall Fling

Vidalia Onion Casserole

5 to 6 Vidalia onions, sliced
1 sleeve Ritz crackers
2 cups grated Parmesan cheese
¾ cup melted butter

Layer onions, crackers and cheese; repeat. Pour melted butter over top. Bake at 350° for 30 to 45 minutes.

Culpeper Air Fest

Claude Moore Colonial Farm

Onion Pie

Served on the farm site.

Pie Crust:

2 cups flour
1 teaspoon salt
⅔ cup butter, chilled
4 to 5 tablespoons cold water

Preheat oven to 350°. Combine flour and salt in large bowl; cut in butter with pastry knife or fork until mixture resembles coarse crumbs. Stir in enough water with fork just until flour is moistened. Divide dough and shape each half into a ball. Flatten 1 ball slightly and roll dough out to fit into a 9-inch pie plate. Roll out second dough ball; set aside.

Filling:

1 large potato, thinly sliced
2 baking apples, thinly sliced
1 large onion, thinly sliced
4 tablespoons butter, divided
6 eggs, divided

¾ teaspoon nutmeg, divided
¾ teaspoon pepper, divided
¾ teaspoon salt, divided
¾ teaspoon mace, divided

Sauté potato, apples and onion with 1 tablespoon butter until soft. In a separate bowl, beat 2 eggs with ¼ teaspoon each nutmeg, pepper, salt and mace. Layer apples, onions, potatoes and egg mixture over prepared pie crust. Beat remaining eggs and pour between layers, sprinkling with remaining spices. Repeat layering until pie is full. Spread remaining butter on top and cover with second pie crust. Cut slits in top crust and bake 1 to 1½ hours or until golden brown.

Claude Moore Colonial Farm

Blue Crab Mac-n-Cheese

2 sticks unsalted butter
½ cup flour
4 cups whole milk
½ to ¾ pound shredded white American
   cheese
¼ tablespoon Parmesan (the sprinkle kind)

1 to 2 tablespoons Old Bay seasoning
Dash Worcestershire sauce
1 pound cavatappi pasta, cooked al dente and
   drained
¾ pound lump backfin crabmeat, or your
   favorite crabmeat

Heat butter and flour in saucepan over low heat. Stir constantly for 3 to 4 minutes or just until it melts, making a light roux. In a separate pot, heat milk until medium-hot but not scalding. Add heated milk to roux and whisk over medium heat until thick and smooth. Add cheeses, seasoning and Worcestershire sauce; mix well. Add sauce to pasta and mix thoroughly. Add crabmeat and toss until well coated. Makes 12 to 14 servings.

Executive Chef Jerry Weihbrecht, Zos
Virginia Beach

Virginia Beach

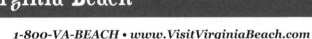

1-800-VA-BEACH • *www.VisitVirginiaBeach.com*

Located in the southeastern tip of the state is famed Virginia Beach. Known for its soft, clean beaches and 3-mile boardwalk, Virginia Beach has endless activities and events throughout the year. Embark on a dolphin-watching boat cruise, grab a kayak and paddle through Back Bay National Wildlife Refuge, learn to hang ten, or simply sit back and relax to the sound of Atlantic waves.

Virginia Beach's fascinating marine life is revealed at the Virginia Aquarium, featuring over 800,000 gallons of aquatic exhibits and the permanent addition Restless Planet, home to 6,000 new animals and 367 new species.

Life at Virginia Beach isn't all sun and sand. Seventeen blocks of shopping, dancing and nightlife can be found at The Town Center. Virginia Beach is also a popular venue for spectacular music festivals, drawing thousands of fans year after year. Enjoy mouthwatering coastal cuisine, with fresh seafood and locally grown produce at every turn.

Spaghetti Aglio, Olio

This is a very simple, fast dinner just right for a warm Summer evening in Tuscany or in Virginia! Pronounced "ah-lee-oh, oh-lee-oh," it means simply "garlic and oil." If you want to do this the real Tuscan way, enjoy the pasta then follow up with a nice salad of mixed field greens dressed just with olive oil and lemon juice and some nice chilled peaches or lemon gelato for dessert.

1 quart salted water
4 tablespoons extra virgin olive oil
6 garlic cloves, minced
1 (12-ounce) package #12 Spaghetti
   (make sure it is durum semolina
   based)

Dried hot pepper flakes to taste,
   optional
2 tablespoons freshly grated aged
   Parmigiano
4 sprigs parsley, freshly chopped

In large pot, bring water to boil. Heat oil in small saucepan; add garlic. Continue heating over medium heat, stirring constantly, 2 minutes, or until garlic begins to slightly brown. Remove from heat immediately and set aside. Add pasta to boiling water. Reduce heat to simmer and cook 10 to 12 minutes. Test pasta toward end of cooking time. It should not be mushy, but should have firm but tender center (al dente). Drain immediately and return to pot. Add garlic mixture and toss well to coat. Add hot pepper, if desired. Serve topped with Parmigiano and parsley.

Delicious paired with Three Fox Vineyard's Volpe Sangiovese or Calabrese Pinot Grigio.

Three Fox Vineyards

Noodle "Thing"

2 tablespoons olive oil
3 tablespoons soy sauce
Garlic salt to taste
Ground ginger to taste
1 can chicken, white meat

1 red bell pepper, sliced
1 head broccoli, cut into pieces
½ bag frozen pea pods
3 packages Ramen noodles

In a saucepan, combine olive oil, soy sauce, garlic salt and ginger over medium heat. Add chicken and pepper slices. Cook 5 minutes. Add broccoli and pea pods; cook until tender, stirring constantly. In separate pan, cook noodles according to package directions, eliminating seasoning packet. Drain water and add to vegetable mixture. Toss and serve.

Lettie Stickley
Grand Caverns

Pasta in Mushroom-Cream Sauce

1 (25-ounce) package frozen cheese or spinach ravioli
2 tablespoons butter
1 (8-ounce) package sliced baby portobello mushrooms
3 green onions, chopped
2 garlic cloves, minced
1 teaspoon dried Italian seasoning
1 (10-ounce) can diced mild tomatoes and green chiles, drained
1 teaspoon dried basil leaves
1 cup whipping cream
½ cup grated Parmesan cheese
½ teaspoon salt
Freshly shaved Parmesan cheese for garnish

Prepare ravioli in a large pot according to directions. Drain and place in a large bowl and keep warm. Melt butter in large Dutch oven over medium-high heat. Add mushrooms, onions, cloves and Italian seasoning. Sauté 9 to 10 minutes or until mushrooms are very tender and slightly browned. Stir in tomatoes and green chiles, basil and whipping cream. Bring to a boil. Reduce heat and simmer 5 minutes, stirring occasionally. Add Parmesan cheese and salt. Add ravioli, tossing to coat. Garnish with freshly shaved Parmesan cheese.

Rita Longworth
Wise County Famous Fall Fling

Mom's Oyster Dressing

1 pint Chincoteague oysters
1½ loaves day old bread
2 teaspoons poultry seasoning
1 small onion, chopped

3 stalks celery, chopped
Turkey essence
Turkey giblets, chopped
Salt and pepper to taste

Drain oysters, reserving juice. Rinse and check oysters for shells. Break bread into pieces and combine with poultry seasoning, onion, celery, turkey essence, and giblets, salt, pepper and reserved juice; mix well. Fold in oysters and spoon mixture into a greased 9x9-inch pan. Bake at 350° for 40 to 45 minutes until dressing is lightly browned on top.

Donna Mason
Chincoteague Island Chamber of Commerce

Chincoteague Island Chamber

Chincoteague • 757-336-6161
www.chincoteaguechamber.com

Chincoteague Island, Virginia's only resort island, is perhaps the most beautiful island on Virginia's Eastern Shore. World famous for its oyster beds and clam shoals, Chincoteague is the gateway to the Assateague Island National Seashore and the Chincoteague National Wildlife Refuge. Adventure awaits everywhere as history and legend blend with the wild loveliness of the seasonal shore. This serene fishing village, seven miles long and one and one-half miles wide and abounding with history and natural charm, welcomes visitors to explore its unique island heritage.

Enjoy world-famous seafood at the Chincoteague Seafood Festival, the first Saturday in May or the Oyster Festival, the Saturday of Columbus Day weekend. Call the chamber or visit their website to learn more about the island and its events.

Fried Vietnamese Egg Rolls

1 pound ground pork
½ cup mashed crabmeat
¾ cup chopped onion
⅓ cup finely chopped black mushrooms
1 teaspoon salt
¼ teaspoon black pepper
10 (8½-inch square) egg roll wrappers, cut in half diagonally
2 egg whites, beaten
Vegetable oil for frying
Romaine lettuce, optional

Combine pork, crabmeat, onion, mushrooms, salt and pepper; set aside. Lay wrapper triangle with point side facing away from you. Place 2 tablespoons stuffing in 3-inch long strip across paper about 2 inches from bottom. Roll partially to enclose filling. Fold right and left edges of wrapper at 45-degree angle to filling, and fold sides toward center. Roll up. Brush edges with a little egg white and seal. Pour 2 inches oil in large pan and heat to medium-high. Fry rolls, a few at a time, 6 minutes or until crisp and golden. Drain on paper towels.

Delicious served with Ming's Mom's Vietnamese Dip Sauce, see next page.

Ming MD
International Children's Festival

Ming's Mom's Vietnamese Dip Sauce

¼ cup water or fresh coconut juice
1 teaspoon rice vinegar
1 teaspoon sugar
1 red chili, seeded and finely chopped
2 garlic cloves, crushed
1 tablespoon lime juice
1 tablespoon fish sauce

Boil water or coconut juice with vinegar and sugar; let cool. In separate bowl, combine chili, garlic and lime juice. Add to coconut mixture. Stir in fish sauce.

Delicious served with Fried Vietnamese Egg Rolls, see previous page.

MingMD
International Children's Festival

Rockingham County Fair

Pad Thai

3 cups medium rice noodles
¼ cup cooking oil
½ cup sliced beef
2 eggs
4 tablespoons fish sauce
4 tablespoons vinegar

1 teaspoon paprika
1 green onion (cut into 1-inch
   lengths)
½ cup bean sprouts
2 tablespoons crushed peanuts
½ teaspoon chili pepper, optional

Soak rice noodles in water 4 hours. In skillet, heat oil over medium-high heat. Add beef, cook until desired doneness. Add eggs, cook until done. Add noodles, fish sauce, vinegar and paprika; mix well. Add green onion, sprouts, peanuts and chili pepper. Continue stirring until noodle is tender but not mushy.

Benji Bes
Representative for Thailand, International Children's Festival

Fried Ripe Plantains

This is a Ghanaian snack.

3 to 4 ripe plantains
Chili pepper to taste
Olive oil for frying

Cut each plantain lengthwise into two parts. Cut each long piece into 1-inch chunks. Place in bowl and rinse under cold water. Sprinkle plantains with chili pepper. Heat oil over medium-high heat and place plantains in oil, turn when golden brown. Remove from oil. Drain on paper towel. Delicious served with peanuts.

Naana Kyereboah
Representative for Ghana, International Children's Festival

Baked Apples with Raisins and Cheese

6 apples
10 ounces plain chevre, Monterey Jack or Gouda cheese
½ cup brown sugar
½ cup raisins
¼ cup slivered blanched almonds, toasted

Core apples and spoon out circular cavity in center. Combine cheese, brown sugar and raisins; mix well. Spoon into hollowed apples and sprinkle with almonds. Bake uncovered at 375° for 45 minutes.

Crossing at the Dan

Breaded Pineapple Casserole

½ cup butter, softened
1 cup sugar
4 eggs
1 teaspoon vanilla extract
1 (14-ounce) can crushed pineapple, drained
5 slices cubed bread (best with bread several days old)

Preheat oven to 350°. Cream butter and sugar together. Beat in eggs, one at a time. Add vanilla and pineapple. Fold in bread cubes. Pour in greased casserole dish and bake 50 minutes.

Faye Matthews
South Hill Wine Festival

Veggie Pizza

2 packages crescent dinner rolls
2 (8-ounce) packages cream cheese, softened
¼ cup mayonnaise
1 package zesty Italian Good Seasons Mix
Chopped veggies (red bell pepper, broccoli, cauliflower, carrots)
1 cup shredded sharp Cheddar cheese

Preheat oven to 375°. Spread crescent rolls on a cookie sheet, pinching ends together to make a large sheet of dough. Bake 7 minutes. Cool. Mix cream cheese, mayonnaise and dressing together. Spread on dough. Sprinkle veggies on top of dressing layer. Top with cheese. Seal and refrigerate overnight. Cut into small squares and serve. Always a hit at parties.

Jackie Beyea
Daffodil Festival

Virginia Beach

Smokin' Stuffing Bites

1½ sticks butter
2 cups diced onions
2 cups diced celery
1 (6-ounce) bag dried cranberries
3 (3-ounce) cans smoked oysters, chopped
3 (6-ounce) boxes turkey- or chicken-flavored stuffing mix
4 cups hot water

In a large pot, melt butter over medium heat. Add onions, celery and cranberries. Cook until desired tenderness. Remove from heat. Add oysters and mix well. Add stuffing mix, stirring well. Add water and continuing mixing. Cover 5 minutes and fluff with fork. Add small amount hot water if too dry or sticky. When cool enough to handle, form into 2- to 3-inch balls and place on greased cookie sheet. Bake at 325° for 12 minutes. Serve warm or room temperature.

Charlotte Chance
Montebello Camping & Fishing Resort

Cheesy Skillet Rice

1 can cream of chicken soup
1½ cups water
½ teaspoon onion powder
½ teaspoon salt
¼ teaspoon pepper
1 cup uncooked white rice
2 cups frozen mixed vegetables
½ cup shredded Cheddar cheese

In medium skillet, combine soup, water, onion powder, salt, pepper and rice; bring to boil. Reduce heat to low, cover and cook 15 minutes, stirring once or twice. Stir in vegetables and cook additional 8 minutes. Top with cheese and cook additional 5 minutes or until rice and vegetables are tender.

Brown Rice & Butter

¾ stick butter
1½ cups Uncle Ben's Converted Rice (no substitutions)
1 can beef bouillon soup

Place butter in bottom of deep casserole dish. Cover with rice and soup. Bake covered 45 minutes at 350°.

Culpeper Air Fest

Cheese Fluff

6 slices bread
1 cup grated cheese, divided
1½ cups milk

2 eggs, beaten
2 tablespoons butter
Paprika to taste

Preheat oven to 350°. Trim bread crust and cut into small cubes. Place ½ bread cubes in bottom of casserole dish. Sprinkle ½ cup cheese on top; repeat. Combine milk and eggs. Pour over bread and cheese. Dot with butter and sprinkle with paprika. Bake 30 minutes.

Stratford Hall

Mini Quiches

½ small purple onion,
   sliced
6 eggs plus 3 egg yolks
½ cup grated Parmesan
   cheese

½ teaspoon salt
½ teaspoon pepper
1½ cups milk
½ cup shredded Swiss
   cheese

Spray mini-muffin pan with non-stick spray. Place 1 to 2 slices onion in bottom of each cup. Combine eggs, yolks, Parmesan, salt, pepper and milk; whisk well. Fill each muffin cup with mixture. Sprinkle each with Swiss cheese. Bake at 350° for 25 minutes.

Creamy Stone Ground Grits

6 cups water
6 cups milk
2 teaspoons salt
1 teaspoon white pepper
4 tablespoons butter, divided
1½ cups stone ground grits
1 pound grated white Cheddar cheese

In a large saucepan, over medium heat, add water, milk, salt, pepper and 2 tablespoons butter; bring to boil. Stir in grits. Cook 1 hour and 15 minutes, stirring frequently (grits will stick to bottom of pan, be sure to scrape bottom). Remove from heat and stir in remaining butter and cheese.

Delicious served with Smothered Andouille Sausage and Shrimp (see page 173).

Virginia Highlands Festival

Brunch Frittatas

20 eggs
2 cups milk
½ red onion, chopped
2 cups spinach
2 cups crumbled feta cheese
Salt and pepper to taste

Preheat oven to 350°. Whisk together eggs and milk. Sauté onion in butter; when slightly soft, add spinach. Pour egg mixture in casserole dish, add spinach and onions, feta cheese, salt and pepper. Cover and bake 45 minutes.

Shaena Muldoon, owner
The Palisades Restaurant

The Palisades Restaurant

168 Village Street • Eggleston
www.thepalisadesrestaurant.com • 540-626-2828

Eggleston, once a thriving and bustling village, is now home to The Palisades Restaurant. Located in the original General Store, known as the Pyne Store, The Palisades Restaurant offers contemporary cuisine in a unique countryside setting, warm hospitality and service in an historic landmark building. The Palisades is truly a neighborhood restaurant – the majority of their pork, beef, trout and produce is grown in the New River Valley, providing guests with the freshest ingredients while supporting the local economy. Fast becoming a destination restaurant, the drive to Eggleston through the beautiful country side enhances the experience.

Sausage & Egg Casserole

A delicious breakfast on its own, or served with grits and fresh seasonal fruit.

1 pound bulk pork sausage
6 eggs
2 cups milk
1 teaspoon salt

1 teaspoon ground mustard
Pepper to taste
6 slices white bread, ½-inch cubes
1½ cups shredded Cheddar cheese

In skillet, brown and crumble sausage; drain and set aside. In large bowl, beat eggs; add milk, salt, mustard and pepper. Spread bread cubes over bottom of greased 11x17-inch baking dish. Layer sausage and cheese atop bread. Pour egg mixture evenly over bread/sausage/cheese layers. Cover and refrigerate 8 hours or overnight. Remove from refrigerator 30 minutes before baking. Bake, uncovered, at 350° for 40 minutes or until a knife inserted near the center comes out clean.

Reynolds Homestead

Reynolds Homestead

463 Homestead Lane • Critz
276-694-7181 • www.reynoldshomestead.vt.edu

The home of Hardin and Nancy Cox Reynolds, built in 1843 as the Rock Spring Plantation, is designated as a State and National Historic Landmark. Hardin Reynolds was a successful farmer, merchant, banker and tobacco manufacturer. He and his children influenced the economic and cultural growth of the United States, particularly in the South. Son R. J. Reynolds founded the R. J. Reynolds Tobacco Company, and grandson Richard Samuel, Sr. founded Reynolds Metals. The 717-acre homestead, deeded to Virginia Tech in 1970, has been authentically restored and is open for tours.

A continuing education center located at the Reynolds Homestead offers educational and cultural programs and performances throughout the year, including a Victorian Christmas celebration in December.

Breakfast Spinach Supreme

10 ounces frozen chopped spinach
1 cup Bisquick baking mix
¼ cup finely chopped onion
¼ cup milk
4 eggs, divided
½ cup grated Parmesan cheese
12 ounces cottage cheese
4 ounces Monterey Jack cheese, cubed
2 garlic cloves, crushed or pressed

Preheat oven to 375°. Grease 9x13-inch baking dish. Thaw and thoroughly drain spinach. Combine baking mix, onion, milk and 2 eggs. Pour into prepared dish. In small bowl combine remaining eggs, spinach, cheeses and garlic. Pour over mixture in baking dish. Bake 35 minutes. Let stand 5 minutes before serving.

May be covered and refrigerated up to 4 hours before baking. Bake refrigerated casserole 40 minutes.

Hunter House Victorian Museum

Breakfast Casserole

1 (1-pound) package bacon
½ to ¾ loaf bread, divided
1 package sliced ham
12 eggs
¼ cup milk
¼ cup onions
¼ cup chopped green bell pepper
Salt and pepper to taste
2 cups shredded cheese

Cook bacon in skillet over medium-high heat; drain, crumble and set aside. Crumble ½ bread loaf in bottom of 9x13-inch pan. Layer ham, remaining breadcrumbs, then bacon. Mix eggs, milk, onions, bell pepper, salt and pepper; pour over layers. Bake 35 minutes at 350°, top with cheese and bake additional 20 minutes.

Faye Rakes
Hillsville Downtown Celebration Series

Ham and Spinach Quiche

1 unbaked pie crust
6 slices deli ham
4 slices Swiss cheese
1 small onion, chopped
1 (10-ounce) package frozen chopped spinach, thawed
6 eggs
1½ cups half and half
Salt and pepper to taste

Preheat oven to 350°. Place uncooked crust in pie dish and press down. Chop deli ham and place in bottom of pie shell. Layer cheese and onion over ham. Squeeze liquid out of spinach and place on top of onion. Beat eggs; blend in half and half and spices. Pour over filling in pie shell. Bake 40 minutes. Quiche is done when knife in center comes out clean. Let stand 10 minutes.

Jackie Beyea
Daffodil Festival

The Edith J. Carrier Arboretum at James Madison University

www.jmu.edu/arboretum/education.shtml

The arboretum invites visitors to enter a world of natural beauty, follow trails through a native oak-hickory forest with beds of wildflowers, and explore nature through lectures, tours, and workshops. With 125 acres of forested slopes, lowland swale, and wetlands, the arboretum preserves and exhibits a habitat diverse in flora and fauna. The arboretum makes a global impact through research and is free to all.

Christine Anderson Photography

Grey Swan Inn Signature Strata

¼ cup mushrooms
¼ cup chopped onions
¼ cup chopped jalapeños
¼ cup chopped roasted peppers
1 tablespoon butter
¼ pound bulk sausage, optional
3 large eggs

½ cup milk
¼ cup Cheddar cheese, shredded
¼ cup Swiss cheese, shredded
¼ cup crumbled feta cheese
1 to 2 cups croutons
Curry powder to taste
4 tablespoons salsa, divided

Preheat oven to 350°. Sauté vegetables in butter; set aside. Brown sausage and drain. In a separate bowl, combine eggs, milk and cheeses; whip thoroughly and set aside. Spray 4 (8-ounce) ramekins with nonstick cooking spray. Place single layer of croutons in each ramekin. Spoon vegetables and sausage over croutons. Add egg mixture over both layers until barely covered. Top with croutons and spoon remaining egg mixture until ramekin is full. Dust with curry powder. Place ramekins on cookie sheet and bake 30 minutes. Loosen strata with rounded knife point and invert onto plate. Garnish each with 1 tablespoon salsa and serve.

Jim and Christine Hasbrouck
The Grey Swan Inn Bed & Breakfast
Blackstone Arts & Crafts Festival

Meat & Seafood

David's Chicken and Dumplings

1 whole chicken
2 tablespoons garlic powder
1 tablespoon kosher salt
½ tablespoon black pepper
½ tablespoon onion powder
3 stalks celery, cut into 2-inch pieces
2 medium onions, chopped
3 garlic cloves, chopped
1 teaspoon red pepper flakes
1 tablespoon Montreal Chicken Seasoning (McCormick)
3 tablespoons cornstarch, dissolved in ¼ cup water

Combine chicken, garlic powder, salt, pepper, onion powder, celery, onions, garlic, red pepper and chicken seasoning in large pot and cover with water. Cook 40 minutes or until chicken falls apart. Remove chicken to cool and debone. Strain liquid and return liquid and deboned chicken to stew pot. Bring back to slow boil. Add cornstarch paste and stir well.

Dumplings:
1½ cups all-purpose flour
1½ cups self-rising flour
1 teaspoon salt
½ teaspoon pepper
4 tablespoons shortening
1¼ cups milk

In bowl, combine flours, salt and pepper. Cut shortening into flour and add milk; mix well. Roll dough out to ½-inch thick and cut into 1x1-inch squares. Add dumplings, dropping in 1 at a time. Simmer, covered, 10 to 15 minutes.

River District Festival

Sun-Dried Tomato Artichoke Chicken

1½ pounds boneless skinless chicken breast
¼ cup Italian breadcrumbs
2 tablespoons olive oil
½ cup chicken broth
Juice of 1 lemon
1 teaspoon dried thyme leaves, divided
1 large (14-ounce) can artichoke hearts, drained
⅓ cup (7½-ounce jar) julienne-cut sun-dried tomatoes in oil
2 tablespoons butter
½ teaspoon salt
⅛ teaspoon pepper
2 tablespoons freshly shaved Parmesan cheese

Preheat large sauté pan on medium high, 2 to 3 minutes. Cut chicken into 1-inch chunks. Place in Ziploc bag and add breadcrumbs. Shake well. Place olive oil in pan, swirl to coat. Add chicken and cook 2 to 3 minutes on each side until chicken begins to brown. Stir in chicken broth, reduce heat to medium-low and cook 2 to 3 minutes or until liquid is slightly reduced. Squeeze juice of lemon over chicken and stir in ½ teaspoon thyme, artichoke hearts, sun-dried tomatoes, butter, salt and pepper. Cover and cook 2 to 3 minutes longer or until done. Remove from heat and stir in remaining thyme. Sprinkle with Parmesan cheese.

Rita Longworth
Wise County Famous Fall Fling

Rosemary Chicken

This recipe is served at Colonial Market Fairs.

1 (4- to 5-pound) whole chicken
3 tablespoons salted butter, softened
1 heaping tablespoon rosemary
2 tablespoons kosher salt

Preheat oven to 425°. Remove giblets from chicken and rinse inside and out; pat dry and set aside. Combine butter, rosemary and salt; mixing thoroughly. Spread butter mixture evenly over chicken skin. With cooking string, tie chicken legs and wings close to body. Place in roasting pan and cook 1½ hours, or until juices run clear. Remove from oven, cover with aluminum foil, and allow to rest about 15 minutes before carving.

Claude Moore Colonial Farm

Crossing at the Dan

Lemon Rosemary Chicken

½ cup fresh lemon juice
⅓ cup olive oil
2 tablespoons chopped shallots
   or green onions
2 tablespoons chopped fresh
   rosemary
½ teaspoon salt
½ teaspoon freshly ground
   black pepper
1 frying chicken, quartered
Handful fresh rosemary springs

Combine lemon juice, oil, shallots, rosemary, salt and pepper; mix well. Place chicken quarters and marinade in plastic food storage bag and seal tightly. Massage bag to distribute marinade. Set in a large bowl and refrigerate at least 2 hours or all day, turning occasionally. Soak rosemary in water for 2 hours or more before cooking. Remove chicken quarters and pat dry; reserve marinade. Place on grill skin side down, turning frequently, 30 to 35 minutes or until done. The last 10 minutes, drop soaked rosemary on fire and brush chicken with marinade.

Crossing at the Dan

Scalloped Chicken

1½ tablespoons butter
⅓ cup slivered almonds
1 envelope onion soup mix
2 tablespoons flour
2 cups milk

1 (16-ounce) can sliced potatoes
1 (16-ounce) can sliced carrots
2 cups cooked and cubed
   chicken
1 cup shredded Cheddar cheese

Preheat oven to 325°. In saucepan, melt butter and cook almonds over medium heat till golden. Stir in soup mix, flour and milk. Reduce heat and simmer, stirring constantly, until mixture is slightly thickened. Drain potatoes and carrots. Layer ½ potatoes, chicken, carrots and prepared sauce in greased casserole dish. Repeat. Bake 25 minutes until hot and bubbly.

Virginia Museum of Contemporary Art

Maple and Garlic Rubbed Chicken

2 tablespoons olive oil
5 boneless, skinless chicken breast halves (cut into bite-size pieces)
2 garlic cloves
½ cup chopped cilantro
2 tablespoons lime juice
Salt and pepper to taste
1 cup maple syrup

Heat oil in large skillet over medium-high heat. Add chicken and brown on all sides. Add garlic and continue cooking until chicken is no longer pink in middle. Stir in cilantro, lime juice, salt and pepper. Add maple syrup. Cook until just heated through. Serve with rice.

Chef John Shields, Gertrude's
Occoquan Craft Fair

Boardwalk Art Show and Festival

June

Since 1956, the Boardwalk Art Show has been a favorite summer event for locals and visitors alike. It features 300 fine artists displaying works in various media and attracts more than 350,000 visitors each year over Father's Day Weekend. Eclectic shopping offers visitors a unique souvenir from Virginia Beach!

Lynn's Family Recipe for Baked Chicken

Chicken can be cut into half breasts, ¼ breast, or bite size pieces for appetizers.

10 to 12 boneless chicken breast halves
1 stick butter, melted
2 cups plain breadcrumbs
¼ cup Parmesan cheese
1 tablespoon crushed basil
1 tablespoon oregano
1 tablespoon garlic salt

Preheat oven to 350°. Coat chicken in butter; set aside. In Ziploc bag, combine breadcrumbs, Parmesan cheese, basil, oregano and garlic salt. Add chicken to bag and shake well, coating chicken. Place chicken in greased, shallow casserole dish. Bake 15 minutes covered with foil. Uncover and bake additional 20 to 25 (adjust cooking time according to size of chicken pieces).

Topping:
1½ sticks butter, softened
1 cup white wine
Green tops of fresh onions to taste
Chopped fresh parsley to taste

Combine all ingredients; mix well. Spoon over chicken and bake additional 15 minutes, uncovered.

Culpeper Air Fest

Crockpot Southwest Chicken

Great served over rice, with cheese and sour cream or in a tortilla with lettuce, tomatoes, cheese and sour cream. Experiment a bit. Works well for lunch the next day too!

6 boneless, skinless chicken breasts
2 (15-ounce) cans fiesta corn
1 (15-ounce) can black beans, drained and rinsed
1 cup minced onion
½ cup minced celery
1 teaspoon garlic powder
Dried cilantro to taste
Seasoned pepper to taste
1 (16-ounce) jar chunky salsa

Place chicken breasts in crockpot. Pour corn, black beans, onion and celery on top of chicken. Sprinkle on garlic powder, cilantro and pepper. Pour salsa over top; cover. Cook on high 5 to 6 hours or until chicken is tender.

Daffodil Festival

Daffodil Festival

April

Historic Court Circle
6467 Main Street • Gloucester
804-693-2355
www.daffodilfestival.org

Every year since 1987, the Gloucester Daffodil Council in coordination with Gloucester Parks, Recreation and Tourism, sponsors a festival to celebrate the daffodil. The festival is a two-day event which starts with a parade down Main Street. Vendors line the street and the court circle offering a wide variety of handcrafts, fine arts and merchandise. A festival queen is selected to represent the festival at other events throughout the year in the county and surrounding area. A poster is designed from artwork submitted by community members and selected by the council to represent the festival. Souvenirs featuring the daffodil are also available every year for purchase. All proceeds from the festival are kept local through county beautification, planting of additional bulbs, a scholarship program for local high school students and support of community activities.

Pasta Bear Knoll

1 pound skinless, boneless
   chicken breasts (cubed)
4 tablespoons olive oil, divided
1 tablespoon oregano
1 tablespoon basil
1 teaspoon marjoram
½ teaspoon anise
½ teaspoon garlic powder
Dash nutmeg

1 teaspoon salt
½ teaspoon pepper
1 green bell pepper
1 red bell pepper
1 large Bermuda onion
2 garlic cloves, minced
1 pint tomatoes
2 cups cooked pasta

Toss chicken with 2 tablespoons olive oil, oregano, basil, marjoram, anise, garlic powder, nutmeg, salt and pepper; mix well. Cover and refrigerate 2 hours. Slice green and red bell peppers into strips. Slice onion into rings. Set aside. Sauté chicken in skillet until done. Remove from skillet and set aside. Sauté bell peppers and onion in remaining olive oil until tender. Add garlic and cook 1 minute. Add tomatoes and chicken and cook 30 minutes. Add pasta, mix well and serve.

Janice Kiehl
The Virginia Lovers' Gourd Society
Virginia Gourd Festival

Aunt Myrtle's Chicken

1 large fryer, skinned, cut into pieces
1 cup milk

¾ cup oil
Flour, seasoned with salt and pepper

Soak chicken in milk 5 minutes. Heat oil in skillet. Coat chicken in seasoned flour and brown on all sides.

Bread Dressing:

9 cups toasted bread, torn into pieces
¾ cup finely chopped celery
¾ cup finely chopped onion
2 tablespoons chopped parsley

1 teaspoon black pepper
2 cups chicken broth
Salt to taste

Preheat oven to 350°. Combine all ingredients and toss. Layer ½ mixture in greased casserole dish, top with chicken and top with remaining mixture. Bake 1½ hours.

Myrtle Bowman
Buckland Farm Market

Buckland Farm Market

Open Monday through Saturday 9am to 7pm and Sundays 9am to 6pm

4484 Lee Highway • New Baltimore
540-341-4739 • www.bucklandfarmmarket.com

Buckland Farm Market is a family-owned and operated country produce market located on a working farm in Fauquier County. The Market offers local produce, supplied from Buckland Farm and other producers. They are known as "the home of the vine-ripened tomato."

On the premises is Sherry Lynn's Bake Shop, offering delicious pies, breads, loaf cakes, cookies, whoopie pies, strudels and turnovers. Each fall there is a challenging 4-acre corn maze and fall festival with farm animals, hayrides around the farm, and other children's activities. And last but not least, there are Christmas trees, wreaths made onsite, garland, poinsettias and old-fashioned Christmas candies available till Christmas Eve. Their motto is true, and says it all.... Always Fresh, Always Friendly!

Mexican Chicken & Rice

1 tablespoon oil
2 pounds boneless, skinless
  chicken breast
1 onion, chopped
1 green bell pepper, chopped
Salt and pepper to taste
1 (8-ounce) package frozen corn,
  thawed

1 cup chicken broth
½ cup salsa
1 cup instant rice
1 cup shredded Cheddar cheese
Sour cream, salsa and cheese for
  garnish

In skillet, heat oil over medium-high heat. Add chicken, onion, bell pepper, salt and pepper; cook until done. Add corn, chicken broth and salsa; bring to a boil. Stir in instant rice. Cover tightly and reduce heat to low and cook 10 minutes. Sprinkle cheese over top, cover, and cook additional 5 minutes. Serve with sour cream, extra salsa and cheese.

Faye Rakes
Hillsville Downtown Celebration Series

Pale Ale Lime Grilled Chicken Sandwich

1 lime, juiced
1 (12-ounce) bottle pale ale style beer
1 teaspoon honey
3 tablespoons chopped cilantro
Salt and pepper to taste
4 skinless, boneless chicken breasts
4 kaiser rolls, toasted
¼ cup prepared coleslaw, optional

Preheat grill to medium heat. Once preheated, brush grate lightly with oil. Mix lime juice, beer, honey, cilantro, salt and pepper. Place chicken in sauce, cover and marinate 30 minutes. Remove from marinade and place on grill. Cook 8 minutes on each side or until juices run clear. Discard leftover marinade. Place chicken on rolls and top with coleslaw.

Blue Ridge Mountain Catering
Blacksburg Fork and Cork

Best Ever Barbecued Chicken

1 chicken fryer, quartered
1 cup ketchup
⅓ cup water
3 tablespoons wine vinegar
1 tablespoon steak sauce
2 drops hot sauce

1 garlic clove, minced
½ teaspoon basil
½ teaspoon oregano
¼ teaspoon thyme
½ teaspoon salt

Wash and pat dry chicken; set aside. Combine ketchup, water, vinegar, steak sauce, hot sauce, garlic, basil, oregano, thyme and salt in saucepan. Bring to boil. Place chicken, skin side up, on grill. Brush chicken with sauce. Turn frequently, basting constantly. Grill 50 to 60 minutes, depending on size of chicken.

Home Craft Days

Home Craft Days
October

Mountain Empire Community College
Big Stone Gap
276-523-7489
www.homecraftdays.org

When Mountain Empire Community College opened its doors in 1972, it served one of the richest areas in the nation for traditional music and crafts. On the faculty were two folklorists, Roddy Moore and George Reynolds, who, with their students, visited musicians and artists throughout Virginia and learned about their music, arts, and mountain life skills. They invited the folks they met to come

to the campus for a celebration of Appalachian culture called Home Craft Days.

For over 38 years musicians and craftspeople from southwest Virginia, east Tennessee, and eastern Kentucky have come to Mountain Empire Community College each October for a celebration they have now made their own. Crafts and demonstrations include weaving, pottery making, grist milling, wood crafting, basket weaving, broom making, quilting, tatting and much more.

Chicken Paprika

1 tablespoon butter
4 boneless, skinless chicken breast halves
1 can cream of chicken soup
⅓ cup sour cream
2 teaspoons paprika
⅛ teaspoon ground red pepper
4 cups hot cooked egg noodles

Heat butter in skillet over medium-high heat. Cook chicken on all sides 10 minutes or until browned. Add soup, sour cream, paprika and pepper; heat to boil. Return chicken to pan. Cover and cook over low heat 5 minutes or until chicken is done. Stir occasionally. Serve over egg noodles.

Trudie Hylton
Virginia Southern Gospel Jubilee

Chicken Tetrazzini

2 cups cooked, diced chicken
1 can cream of mushroom soup
1 can cream of chicken soup
3 tablespoons parsley
1 (3-ounce) can mushrooms

½ stick butter, melted
Salt and pepper to taste
12 ounces spaghetti, cooked and
   drained
Grated Cheddar cheese

Combine all ingredients, except cheese, in a 2-quart casserole dish. Top with cheese. Bake at 350° for 15 minutes.

Linda Phillips
General's Ridge Vineyard

General's Ridge Vineyard

Cerveza Wings

1½ pounds chicken wings or drumettes
1 teaspoon salt
1 teaspoon dried thyme
1 teaspoon red pepper flakes
½ teaspoon black pepper
1 (12-ounce) bottle favorite Mexican cerveza (beer)

Cut off and discard wing tips. Cut each wing in half at joint. Place chicken in shallow bowl; sprinkle with seasonings. Pour beer over chicken; toss to coat. Cover and refrigerate 3 hours. Preheat oven to 375°. Line shallow baking pan with foil; spray with nonstick cooking spray. Drain chicken, reserving marinade. Arrange chicken on prepared pan in single layer. Bake 40 minutes or until chicken is well browned on all sides, turning and basting with reserve marinade occasionally. Discard remaining marinade.

Chef Randall Spencer
Blue Ridge Mountain Catering
Blacksburg Fork and Cork

Roast Turkey with Goat Cheese and Shiitake Mushroom

Delicious paired with DuCard Vineyard's Signature Viognier

¼ cup prepared pesto
8 thin slices Ciabatta bread
8 ounces sliced roast turkey breast
4 ounces sliced shiitake mushrooms, sautéed

1 roasted red bell pepper, stemmed, skinned,
  seeded (cut into thin strips)
4 ounces goat cheese
1 tablespoon extra-virgin olive oil

Spread pesto evenly on 4 bread slices. Divide turkey, mushrooms, roasted pepper strips and goat cheese equally among remaining 4 bread slices. Top with pesto bread slices, making 4 sandwiches. Brush outsides lightly with olive oil. Heat large skillet, griddle or grill pan over medium-high heat. Add sandwiches and cook 4 minutes or until golden brown and cheese melts, pressing occasionally with a large spatula. Remove sandwiches and transfer to cutting board. Slice in half diagonally; serve immediately.

The Madison Inn · 540-948-5095 · www.madisoninnva.com

DuCard Vineyards

DuCard Vineyards

40 Gibson Hollow Lane • Etlan
540-923-4206 • www.ducardvineyards.com

DuCard Vineyards is a new boutique winery at the edge of Shenandoah National Park, with extensive patios featuring views of mountains, streams and vineyards.

The nearby area includes hiking, fishing, restaurants, bed and breakfasts, historic sites and antique shops, making it an outstanding choice for a country getaway only 90 minutes from the DC Beltway, 90 minutes from Richmond and less than an hour from Charlottesville.

DuCard Vineyards is one of Virginia's leading 'green' wineries, solar powered, built with reclaimed lumber from 100 year old barns on the property, and featuring only local Virginia farmers and producers for the baguettes, cheese, chocolate and other foods available to accompany the wines.

The 7-acre vineyard, meticulously nurtured and tended by hand, produces Viognier, Cabernet Franc and other wines that reflect the rocky soils and rugged character of Madison County.

Stop by for music on the patio, winemaker dinners, festivals or special events.

Mozzarella Stuffed Turkey Burger

1 pound ground turkey
¼ cup finely chopped scallions
2 teaspoons minced garlic
2 teaspoons Worcestershire sauce
1 teaspoon lemon zest
½ teaspoon dried oregano
½ teaspoon pepper
½ teaspoon salt, divided

½ cup shredded mozzarella
  cheese, divided
2 tablespoons finely chopped
  fresh basil
2 teaspoons olive oil
1 (8-ounce) jar marinara sauce,
  divided
4 focaccia bread buns, toasted

In large bowl, combine turkey, scallions, garlic, Worcestershire sauce, lemon zest, oregano, ½ teaspoon pepper and ¼ teaspoon salt; mix gently, being careful not to over mix. Form into 8 thin patties. Combine ¼ cup cheese and basil. Place equal amount cheese mixture in center of 4 patties. Cover with remaining patties and seal edges. Heat oil in large nonstick skillet over medium heat. Add burgers and cook 8 to 10 minutes, turning once. Remove and set aside. Warm marinara and place 3 tablespoons on 1 side of bread. Top with burger, 3 additional tablespoons marinara and 1 tablespoon of remaining cheese.

Chef Randall Spencer
Blue Ridge Mountain Catering
Blacksburg Fork and Cork

Sloppy Joes

1½ pounds ground beef　　⅓ cup mustard
⅓ cup ketchup　　　　　　⅓ cup molasses

Brown ground beef and drain. Mix ketchup, mustard, and molasses. Stir into ground beef and heat through. Serve on hamburger buns.

Sandee Burt, Moneta
Smith Mountain Lake

Prince William County

Formed in 1731, Prince William County has a rich history. Three major battles of the Civil War were fought there, and today, the county is home to two national parks, one state park and dozens of historic sites. Prince William County is a thriving suburb of Washington, DC and is the home of the United States Marine Corps.

Sloppy Joes

1 pound ground beef
1 small onion, chopped
½ cup ketchup

1 tablespoon mustard
1 tablespoon vinegar
1 teaspoon sugar

Brown ground beef and onion; drain. Add ketchup, mustard, vinegar and sugar. Cook over medium heat for 10 minutes, stirring occasionally. Serve on toasted buns.

Jackie Erickson
Ben Lomond

Ben Lomond

Open for tours from May thru October
Thursday to Sunday, 11am to 4pm or by appointment.

10321 Sudley Manor Dr. • Manassas, VA 20109
703-367-7872 • www.pwcgov.org/benlomond

Constructed in 1832, Ben Lomond was the home site of one of the most famous families in Virginia. With an original slave quarter, dairy, and smokehouse still standing, Ben Lomond's history as a wealthy plantation that raised thousands of Merino sheep is still visible today. In July 1861, passing Confederate soldiers converted the house into a temporary field hospital, treating the wounded from the Battle of 1st Manassas. Later in the War, the house was ransacked by passing Federal soldiers, who left graffiti and destroyed furniture, many of which remain today. Ben Lomond is open to the public, its appearance preserved since the 1800's.

(See page 196 for a list of historic sites near Ben Lomond.)

Blue Cheese & Bacon Stuffed Burger

4 slices applewood smoked bacon
1 red onion, finely chopped
2 tablespoons crumbled blue cheese
½ teaspoon salt
½ teaspoon pepper
1 teaspoon Worcestershire sauce
1½ pounds ground sirloin

Cook bacon in skillet over medium-high heat until chewy; drain. Chop into small pieces. In same skillet, add onion and cook until soft. Spread onto plate to cool. In a small bowl, combine bacon, onion, blue cheese, salt, pepper and Worcestershire. Blend well. Divide ground sirloin into four, ¾-cup pieces. Place 1 piece on cutting board; divide in half. Flatten each half into thin patty about 4-inches wide. Place 1 tablespoon bacon mixture in center of one patty; cover with other patty. Pinch edges together to seal. Shape burger until round and slightly flattened. Repeat with remaining burger and bacon mixture. Grill on medium hot 4 to 6 minutes per side or until desired doneness. Let stand 2 minutes before serving.

Blue Ridge Mountain Catering
Chef Randall Spencer
Blacksburg Fork and Cork

Old-Fashioned Meatloaf

1½ pounds ground chuck
2 eggs
¼ teaspoon salt
¼ teaspoon pepper
¼ cup chopped onions

½ cup chopped green bell
  peppers
1 cup tomato sauce
1 cup instant oatmeal

Preheat oven to 350°. Mix all ingredients. Shape into loaf and bake 1 hour.

Faye Rakes
Hillsville Downtown Celebration Series

Mountain Meadow Farm

Sweet and Sour Meatballs

2 pounds lean ground beef
1 medium onion, finely chopped
1 medium green bell pepper, finely chopped
2 eggs
¼ teaspoon salt
½ teaspoon cinnamon
½ teaspoon allspice
½ teaspoon black pepper
⅓ cup plain breadcrumbs

Heat oven to 400°. In a large bowl, mix beef, onions, bell pepper, eggs, seasonings and breadcrumbs. Form into 1-inch balls. Place in an ungreased 9x13-inch baking dish. Bake uncovered 20 minutes or until meatballs are no longer pink in center.

Sweet & Sour Sauce:
2 cups ketchup
1 cup brown sugar
1 cup pineapple juice
2 tablespoons cornstarch
1 (16-ounce) can pineapple, drained

In a 2-quart saucepan, combine all ingredients. Over medium high-heat, bring to a boil, stirring occasionally. Reduce heat and cover; simmer 15 minutes. Add meatballs. Serve warm with toothpicks.

Sheila Matthew
Blackstone Arts & Crafts Festival

Meatballs

1½ pounds ground beef
3 tablespoons Worcestershire sauce
½ teaspoon pepper
¾ cup crushed crackers

3 to 4 tablespoons chopped onion
2 bell peppers, cored, seeded (sliced wide)

Combine all ingredients except bell peppers. Roll into small balls and brown. Drain.

Sauce:

2 tablespoons A1 steak sauce
2 tablespoons Worcestershire sauce
2 tablespoons sugar
1 cup water

6 to 8 tablespoons chopped onions
1½ cups ketchup
3 tablespoons white vinegar

Combine all ingredients and mix well; set aside. Line 9x13-inch dish with bell peppers. Place meatballs on top. Pour sauce over peppers and meatballs. Bake at 350° for 45 minutes.

Tressia Boyd
Richlands Fall Festival

Richlands Fall Festival

October

1921 Front Street
Richlands
276-964-1711
www.richlands-events.com

Usher in the fall season in Richlands at the annual Richlands Fall Festival. This day-long celebration is complete with arts, crafts, food, music and more. Local stores get in on the action, offering discounts and giveaways throughout the weekend. There are children's activities, bus ridges, and a 5K Road Race and Fun Run. A delightful day in a charming town is what the Richlands Fall Festival is all about.

Barnstormer's Noodle Surprise

1 pound ground beef
1 small onion, chopped
12 ounces noodles, cooked and drained
1 can cream of mushroom soup
1 soup can hot water
Cheese slices
Salt and pepper to taste

Brown hamburger and onion; drain. Layer hamburger and noodles alternately in baking dish. Pour mushroom soup and water over all. Cover with cheese slices. Bake at 350° for 40 minutes.

Flying Circus Airshow

Flying Circus Airshow
Sundays—May through October

Located just off Route 17
at 5114 Ritchie Road
Bealeton
540-439-8661
www.flyingcircusairshow.com

The Flying Circus Airshow features a host of antique airplanes including Stearmans, WACOs, Fleets, Cubs, Champs, and others. Performances include formation flying demonstrations, world class aerobatics, death-defying wing walkers, classic comedy routines and more providing an afternoon of fun for the whole family. Airplane
rides are available for purchase both before and after the Sunday performance. These include open cockpit rides in the historic Stearman biplane, double rides for two in an antique WACO biplane, and kid's rides in the famous Piper Cub. Extreme aerobatic biplane rides are also available to the most adventurous spirits. For more information including admission, airplane ride prices, and a detailed schedule of events, please see visit their website.

Vernon Wells

Broiled Hamburg Steak on Onion Rings

First appeared in The Southern Planter *magazine, October 1937*

7 slices Spanish onion, ½-inch thick
3 tablespoons butter, divided
Salt and pepper to taste
1 tablespoon water
1 tablespoon chopped parsley
2 cups ground beef
¼ cup ground suet*
1 cup soft fine breadcrumbs
7 strips bacon
3 tablespoons butter
2 teaspoons onion juice

Preheat oven to 350°. Place onion slices in greased shallow baking dish. Melt 2 tablespoons butter and pour over onions, sprinkle with salt and pepper. Add water, cover loosely, and bake 30 minutes or until tender. In skillet, heat remaining butter, add parsley, beef, suet, breadcrumbs, salt and pepper. Cook until thoroughly mixed. Mold into 7 flat cakes and wrap each with slice bacon. Place each cake on onion slice in baking dish. Broil under direct heat 5 minutes on each side, basting occasionally with drippings. Serve immediately.

*Modern cooks may not keep suet in their refrigerators, but there is no true substitute for this particular type of animal fat. Your butcher should be able to provide it, but if you must replace the suet, solid vegetable shortening is acceptable.

Janet L. Cameron, Virginia Food and Nutrition Specialist
Morven Park

Cottage Pie

1½ pounds ground beef
1 large onion, finely chopped
3 carrots, peeled and sliced
2 tablespoons flour
Salt and pepper to taste
1 cup beef bouillon

2 tablespoons Worcestershire
  sauce
1 pound potatoes
3 tablespoons butter
Milk or cream

Preheat oven to 375°. Crumble ground beef into skillet with onion and carrots. Cook until beef is well done; drain. In same skillet add flour, salt and pepper. Mix well. Add beef bouillon and Worcestershire sauce. Cover and simmer 30 minutes. While beef is simmering, peel and quarter potatoes and boil until tender. Drain potatoes and mash with butter and milk to suit. Transfer meat and carrots to an oven proof dish. Top with mashed potatoes. Top potatoes with additional butter. Bake 20 minutes at 375°, brown under hot broiler if desired.

Hunter House Victorian Museum

Wild Rice Casserole

2 tablespoons butter	1 pound ground beef
¼ chopped onion	1 cup wild rice
¼ cup chopped green bell pepper	Salt and pepper to taste
	3 cups beef broth

Preheat oven to 350°. Melt butter in skillet. Sauté onion and bell pepper until tender. Add ground beef and brown. Add rice and sauté an additional 5 minutes. Place beef mixture in greased casserole dish. Season with salt and pepper. Pour broth over top. Bake, covered, 1½ hours or until rice is tender.

South Hill Ruritan Club
Antique Farm Machinery and Vehicle Show

Swiss Steak

Don't let "Swiss" in the title fool you. This hearty dish feeds even the hungriest cowboy, deliciously. Though we traditionally serve it over mashed potatoes, this is good over noodles and rice, too.

1½ pounds beef round steak
  (¾-inch thick)
2 tablespoons flour
1 teaspoon Kosher salt
¼ teaspoon pepper
3 teaspoons garlic powder
2 teaspoons vegetable oil
1 (16-ounce) can diced stewed
  tomatoes

1 large sweet onion, sliced
2 stalks celery, thinly sliced
2 medium carrots, diced
1 (8-ounce) jar sliced mushrooms,
  optional
1 tablespoon Worcestershire sauce
½ cup beef stock
1 to 2 tablespoons cornstarch

Preheat oven to 325°. Combine all ingredients, except cornstarch, in a large covered baking dish. Bake 2 hours; stir in cornstarch. Bake another 1 hour or until done. Serve hot over mashed potatoes.

Oakland Heights Farm

The Madison Inn's Steak Diane

Pairs with DuCard Vineyards Popham Run Red

12 ounces sliced beef tenderloin
½ teaspoon salt
¼ teaspoon freshly ground black
   pepper
1 tablespoon unsalted butter
2 teaspoons chopped shallots

1 teaspoon minced garlic
1 cup sliced baby bella
   mushrooms
¼ cup Cognac or brandy
2 teaspoons Dijon mustard
¼ cup beef stock

Season beef with salt and pepper. Melt butter in large skillet over medium-high heat. Add beef and cook 45 seconds on the first side, turn and cook 30 seconds. Add shallots and garlic to side of pan and cook 20 seconds, stirring constantly. Add mushrooms cook 2 minutes. Place beef on plate and cover. Remove pan from heat. Tilt pan towards you and add brandy. Tip pan away from you and ignite brandy with match. Return to heat. When flame has burned out, add mustard and cook 1 minute. Add beef stock and simmer 1 minute. Return beef and any accumulated juices to pan, coating beef with sauce and juices.

The Madison Inn · 540-948-5095 · www.madisoninnva.com

DuCard Vineyards

DuCard Vineyards

Sue's House Steak Marinade

1 cup soy sauce
¾ cup pancake syrup
½ cup vinegar
¾ teaspoon garlic powder

2 teaspoons ginger
1¼ tablespoons onion powder
3 cups oil

Combine all ingredients and blend well.

Dan & Sue Harshman
Edinburg Mill

Pigg River Ramble Weekend

May

**On the Blackwater and Pigg Rivers
Franklin County
540-483-9293
www.visitfranklincountyva.org**

Held annually in May, the Pigg River Ramble Weekend combines 2 rivers for 3 days of fun. Friday night kicks off the weekend with a night-time float on the Blackwater River. Promoted as the Blackwater Blackout this event draws out the most daring boaters for a fun 2 mile float down the river in complete darkness. Participants arrive at the put in and enjoy a BBQ meal and music before nightfall, and when the lights go out down the river they go. Bright and early the next day begins the annual Pigg River Ramble Race and Float. The Pigg River Ramble is a seven mile race down the Pigg River. Racers are divided into categories—canoe, kayak, tandem, and solo. Participants are of all ages and it is truly a family affair. All participants receive the ever popular Pigg River Ramble T-Shirt (a collector's item) and the best BBQ meal in Southwest Virginia. The last day it's back to the Blackwater River with Breakfast on The Blackwater. This laid back Sunday float is just what everyone needs to bring this three-day action-packed weekend to a close.

Venison Loin with Blueberry Butter Sauce

Venison loin

Wash venison loin and pat dry; set aside

Marinade:

1 bottle red wine	2 celery ribs
1 pint fresh blueberries	3 to 4 bay leaves
2 carrots, chopped	Fresh thyme
1 onion, chopped	

Combine all ingredients and mix well. Marinate venison two days (refrigerated).

Salt and pepper to taste	1 onion, diced
1 tablespoon olive oil	2 celery ribs, diced
1 tablespoon butter	Bay leaves
2 carrots, diced	Fresh thyme

Preheat oven to 350°. Remove venison from marinade, reserving liquid. Season venison with salt and pepper. Heat olive oil and butter in skillet over medium-high heat. Sear venison until loin is browned on all sides. Place roasting pan and add carrots, onions, celery, bay and thyme. Roast about 30 minutes (until desired doneness).

Blueberry Butter Sauce:

1 cup heavy cream	1 pound sweet butter

Simmer reserved marinade until reduced to about one cup liquid. Add heavy cream. Reduce again to 1 cup. Strain and return to high heat while whisking in one pound whole cold butter (just prior to serving). Let venison rest prior to carving. Serve with Blueberry Butter Sauce.

Chef John C. Schopp
Pigg River Ramble Weekend

Meat Roll with Stuffing

1 pound ground beef
½ pound pork sausage
1 egg, beaten
1 small onion
4 tablespoons margarine
4 slices bread, cubed
½ cup chopped celery

½ cup raisins
1 teaspoon salt
¼ teaspoon pepper
1 teaspoon sage
1 tablespoon water
4 to 5 slices raw bacon

Mix together beef, sausage and egg. Pat on wax paper in rectangles 1½-inches thick. Sauté onion in margarine and mix with bread, celery, raisins, salt, pepper, sage and water. Roll as a jelly roll. Wind bacon around roll. Cook in 350° oven approximately 1 hour.

Abigail Kime
BW Country Store

Big Walker Lookout

Sausage Casserole

2 pounds sausage
1 cup chopped onion
2 cups cooked rice
6 eggs
2 cans cream of celery soup
2 cups grated mild Cheddar cheese
6 cups Rice Krispies
½ cup milk

Preheat oven to 350°. Brown sausage and drain. Add onion and splash of water. Cook until onion is tender. Add rice; pour into greased 9x13-inch pan. In separate bowl, beat eggs and soup together. Stir in cheese, cereal and milk. Spread over sausage mixture. Cover with foil and bake 45 minutes. Remove foil and bake until brown.

Rachel Morris, The Bodacio
The Bodacious Bazaar & Art Festival

Zesty Pork

3 to 4 pound boneless pork
shoulder
2½ teaspoons salt
1½ teaspoon chili powder

¾ teaspoon cumin
¾ teaspoon oregano
1 large onion, sliced thick
3 cloves garlic

Trim fat from pork and cut into large pieces. Place in slow cooker and add spices, onion and garlic. Cook on low 6 hours or until pork is tender. Shred for sandwiches or burritos.

Fun Fact

"Sic Semper Tyrannis" ...
Thus Always to Tyrants.

This Latin phrase is a rallying cry against the abuse of power, and the two figures represented on the Virginia state flag are acting out the motto. The female warrior, named Virtue, represents Virginia. She stands victorious over the fallen male warrior, the symbol of the tyrant.

Pork & Chorizo Burger

½ pound smoked chorizo sausage, fully cooked and
   casings removed (cut into 1-inch pieces)
1½ pounds ground pork
2 garlic cloves, minced
2 teaspoons Worcestershire sauce
1½ teaspoons Cajun seasoning
¾ teaspoon coarse salt
¼ teaspoon cayenne pepper
4 slices pepper jack cheese
4 ciabatta rolls
½ cup green-chili mayonnaise
Romaine lettuce

Heat grill to medium. In food processor, process chorizo until finely chopped. Place in large bowl and add ground pork, garlic, Worcestershire and seasonings; mix gently. Form mixture into 4 patties. Grill, covered, until cooked through, 7 to 8 minutes per side. Top with cheese and place burger on bun topped with green-chili mayonnaise and lettuce.

Chef Randall Spencer
Blue Ridge Mountain Catering
Blacksburg Fork and Cork

Spanish Pork Burger

1 tablespoon olive oil
2 Spanish onions, thinly sliced
½ teaspoon salt, divided
½ teaspoon pepper, divided
1½ pounds ground pork
1 tablespoon finely chopped
   Spanish green olives
2 teaspoons minced garlic
2 teaspoons smoked paprika
¼ cup mayonnaise

2 teaspoons grated lemon zest
1 tablespoon lemon juice
Pinch saffron
¼ cup shredded Monterey Jack
   cheese
4 whole-wheat hamburger buns,
   toasted
2 piquillo peppers, halved
   lengthwise

In large skillet, heat oil over medium heat. Add onion, ⅛ teaspoon salt and ¼ teaspoon pepper. Cover and cook, stirring occasionally, 10 minutes or until soft and translucent. Set aside half for topping; finely chop remaining half. Preheat grill to medium. In large bowl combine chopped onion, pork, olives, garlic, paprika, and remaining salt and pepper. Gently mix. Form into 4 equal patties, about ½-inch thick. Combine mayonnaise, lemon zest, lemon juice and saffron in small bowl. Place patties on oiled grill rack and cook 8 to 10 minutes, turning once. Top with cheese and cook until melted. Place burgers on buns with lemon-saffron mayonnaise, reserved onions and ½ piquillo pepper.

Chef Randall Spencer
Blue Ridge Mountain Catering
Blacksburg Fork and Cork

Virginia Pulled Pork BBQ

Boston Butt Pork Roast (size to fit in slow cooker)
Ginger Ale, to cover
Salt to taste

Place Boston Butt in slow cooker, covering completely with ginger ale. Add salt. Cook 10 hours. Remove and pull apart, discarding identifiable fat. Keep warm (but do NOT ever microwave) and serve with fresh coleslaw and your choice BBQ sauce. Freezes and reheats well on top of stove with a little added water, white wine or ginger ale. Do not microwave to reheat, it will dry and toughen the meat.

Gail C. Ratliffe
The Virginia Lovers' Gourd Society
Virginia Gourd Festival

Herb-Crusted Roast Pork

½ cup fine, dry breadcrumbs
⅓ cup chopped fresh basil
3 tablespoons olive oil
1 tablespoon freshly ground pepper

1 teaspoon kosher salt
3 tablespoons chopped fresh thyme
1 pound pork tenderloin

Stir together breadcrumbs, basil, olive oil, pepper, salt and thyme. Moisten pork tenderloin with water; press crumb mixture over tenderloin and place on rack. Bake at 425° for 45 minutes or until a meat thermometer inserted in thickest part of tenderloin registers 160°.

Nicole Schermerhorn, owner, A Thyme to Plant Herb Farm
Herbs Galore & More at Maymont

Herbs Galore & More at Maymont

Richmond
804-358-7166
www.maymont.org/herbsgalore

Herbs Galore & More is a gardening extravaganza with more than 50 plant and craft vendors from the mid-Atlantic region selling herbs, annuals, perennials, heirloom plants, vegetables, trees, herbal cosmetics, garden ornaments, and other related products. Meet the Experts sessions offer great inspiration for growing and using herbs, and local restaurants serve up a variety of flavorful food including breakfast treats, luncheon fare, herbal delicacies and vegetarian cuisine. The

event benefits Maymont, a 100-acre American estate featuring the 33-room Maymont Mansion, historic gardens and animal exhibits in Richmond.

Lavender Jelly Pork Roast

Lavender Jelly:
1 cup apple jelly
1 teaspoon culinary lavender buds

Warm apple jelly in saucepan. When dissolved, add lavender buds. Steep 5 minutes. Strain and discard lavender buds.

Pork Roast:
½ teaspoon salt
½ teaspoon garlic salt
½ teaspoon onion powder
4 pound pork roast
1 cup lavender jelly
1 cup ketchup
¼ cup honey
2 tablespoons vinegar

Combine salts and onion powder. Rub over pork. Roast at 325° for 2 hours. In saucepan, combine jelly, ketchup, honey and vinegar; bring to boil. Reduce to simmer, allow to thicken. Brush glaze on pork final 30 minutes cooking time. Add pork drippings to remaining sauce, heat to boiling and serve with pork.

White Oak Lavender Farm

Honey Pork Tenderloin Tailgate Kabobs

½ cup bourbon (may substitute with 2
tablespoons cider vinegar)
½ cup honey
½ cup mustard
1 teaspoon dried tarragon
3 to 4 sweet potatoes, cut into 24 (1-inch)
cubes
1½ pounds pork tenderloin, cut into
24 (1-inch) cubes

4 medium ripe peaches, unpeeled,
pitted and quartered
4 green bell peppers, each cut into
8 (2-inch) pieces
8 yellow onion, each cut into 4 (2-inch)
pieces
8 skewers
Olive oil for grilling

Combine bourbon, honey, mustard and tarragon; stir well and set aside. Boil sweet potatoes until crisp-tender. Thread 3 sweet potato cubes, 3 pork cubes, 2 peach quarters, 4 bell pepper pieces and 4 onion pieces alternately onto each skewer. Brush kabobs with honey glaze mixture. Lightly oil grill. Grill over medium-hot coals 5 minutes on each side or until thoroughly heated, basting occasionally with glaze.

Hampton Heat 200

Hampton Heat 200

July

Langley Speedway
www.langley-speedway.com

One of Langley Speedway's largest annual races, the Hampton Heat occurs every July as Hampton's annual Founder's Day celebration. Doors open at 5:30 pm and festivities at the track culminate with the 200-lap (79-mile) Hampton Heat NASCAR Whelen All-American Late Model Division Stock Car event. A longtime member of the NASCAR Whelen All-American Series and a NASCAR Home Track, Langley Speedway is a .395-mile, slightly-

banked oval. Participating drivers vie for the checkered flag on the track where racing greats Darrell Waltrip, Dale Earnhardt Sr., and Denny Hamlin began their careers. Drivers from throughout the Mid-Atlantic and Southeast come to Hampton to participate in this annual event with the winning driver receiving a large cash prize. In addition to the Late Model division event, Langley Speedway runs racing events for other divisions including Grand Stock, Super Trucks, Legends and UCar, among others. Visit the website for schedule and details.

Pan Seared Pork Tenderloin with Mixed Berry Relish

3 cups mixed berries (sliced strawberries, blackberries, raspberries, blueberries)
1 tablespoon Canola oil
1 pork tenderloin, trimmed
2 cups port wine
¼ cup sugar
½ cup papaya or mango
2 tablespoons fresh mint, chopped
1 tablespoon fresh sage
Salt and pepper to taste

Preheat oven to 400°. Rinse berries well and set aside to drain. In skillet, heat oil over medium-high heat and sear tenderloin on all sides. Place tenderloin in pan and bake 20 minutes or until an internal temperature of 155° is reached.

Pour wine and sugar in saucepan and reduce until consistency of syrup is reached. Combine berries and papayas and remaining ingredients. Pour port reduction around sides of fruit and mix gently until combined.

Slice tenderloin and top with berry relish.

Blacksburg Fork and Cork

Grilled Pork Loin

½ **pork loin**
Mrs. Dash Original Seasoning
Pepper
Italian dressing

Season pork loin with Mrs. Dash and pepper and place on grill at 275° till loin is browned. Remove from grill, slice loin and place on a sheet of aluminum foil. Pour Italian dressing over loin; wrap. Put back on grill and cook till desired doneness. Serve with your favorite grilled vegetables.

Kenny Pittman
Pork, Peanut & Pine Festival

Golf courses with fantastic views of the Virginia Coastline are a favorite for locals and tourists.

thinkstockphotos.com

Orange Glazed Pork Chops

1 (4-ounce) jar Orange Marmalade from The Country Canner
2 tablespoons orange juice
2 tablespoons mustard
1 tablespoon soy sauce
½ teaspoon minced garlic
¼ teaspoon red pepper flakes
4 pork chops
1 teaspoon vegetable oil
½ teaspoon salt
¼ teaspoon pepper

In small bowl, combine orange marmalade, orange juice, mustard, soy sauce, minced garlic and pepper flakes; set aside. In large skillet, brown pork chops in oil on both sides, sprinkle with salt and pepper. Cook uncovered 10 minutes or until done. Remove and keep warm. Add marmalade mixture to skillet and bring to boil. Reduce heat; simmer uncovered for 3 to 4 minutes or until thickened. Spoon sauce over pork chops.

The Country Canner

Dry Rub for Rosemary Pork Chops

1 cup rosemary
¼ cup thyme
3 tablespoons paprika
2 tablespoons Old Bay
  Seasoning

3½ tablespoons chicken
  seasoning
1 tablespoon white pepper
2 tablespoons salt

Mix ingredients together. Will coat approximately 15 pork chops.

James Moore, head cook January - May 2009
The Palisades Restaurant

Weird Laws

• Children are not to go trick-or-treating on Halloween.

• It is illegal to tickle women.

• In Prince William County, no person may keep a skunk as a pet... (This one doesn't really seem that weird, actually.)

• No animal may be hunted on Sunday with the exception of raccoons, which may be hunted until 2am.

• In Norfolk, spitting on a sea gull is not tolerated.

• It is illegal to use profanity on Atlantic Avenue or the boardwalk while in Virginia Beach.

Bacon Baked Rabbit

1 cup flour
2 teaspoons black pepper
2 teaspoons garlic powder
1 tablespoon paprika
Salt to taste
1 rabbit, cut in 5 to 7 pieces
1 cup rendered bacon fat
1 cup fine dry breadcrumbs
Sage, basil or oregano

Preheat oven to 350°. Combine flour, pepper, garlic powder, paprika and salt. Lightly coat rabbit in seasoned flour, shaking off excess. Dip pieces in warm bacon fat, allowing excess to drip off. Coat in breadcrumbs. Arrange rabbit in baking dish. Bake 30 minutes, turn, bake 30 minutes longer. Rabbit will be brown and crisp when done.

Mountain Meadow Farm

Fruit and Walnut Stuffed Wild Striped Bass

¼ cup dried cherries
¼ cup organic raisins
1 onion, chopped
¼ cup melted butter
¼ cup chopped walnuts
2 garlic cloves, sliced
2 tablespoons chopped parsley
2 to 3 pound filet of Striped Bass or any freshwater fish
Freshly ground salt and pepper to taste
1 tablespoon olive oil

Soak cherries and raisins in water 15 minutes or until plumped; drain. Preheat oven to 400°. Combine raisins, cherries, onions, butter, walnuts, garlic and parsley; mix well. Set aside. Season fish with salt and pepper. Line large pan with foil. Brush fish with olive oil and place on foil. Slice fish lengthwise, making sure not to cut all the way through. Stuff opening with fruit mixture, wrap foil loosely and bake 20 to 30 minutes.

Roya Gharavi
Gourmet Pantry & Cooking School
Blacksburg Fork and Cork

Monkfish in Lemon Butter Wine Sauce

1½ pounds Monkfish
Freshly ground salt and pepper to taste
2 tablespoons olive oil
½ cup butter
1 shallot, minced
2 garlic cloves, minced
Juice from one lemon
¼ cup white wine
1 tablespoon parsley

Pat fish dry and season salt and pepper; set aside. Warm olive oil and butter in skillet. When butter is melted, increase temperature to medium-high and add fish. Sauté 3 minutes on each side or until golden brown. Fish should flake apart with fork when done. Remove fish and set aside. While skillet is still hot, add shallots and garlic. Sauté 1 minute or until tender (do not allow garlic to burn). Add lemon juice and wine. Simmer 1 minute. Cut fish into 1-inch pieces and add to sauce with parsley, salt and pepper. Serve with pasta or green vegetables.

Roya Gharavi
Gourmet Pantry & Cooking School
Blacksburg Fork and Cork

Pan-Sautéed Rockfish with Country Ham and Peanut Pesto

Peanut Pesto:

3 cups fresh basil leaves, stems removed, loosely packed

¾ cup roasted, unsalted Virginia peanuts

3 garlic cloves, peeled

¼ cup freshly grated Parmesan cheese

¼ cup freshly grated Romano cheese

¼ teaspoon red pepper flakes

½ teaspoon kosher or sea salt

1 tablespoon fresh lemon juice

⅔ cup extra virgin olive oil

Place basil leaves in food processor or blender; process until well-chopped, scraping side as necessary. Add peanuts, garlic, Parmesan, Romano, red pepper flakes and salt, processing until well chopped and blended. In a small bowl, whisk together lemon juice and olive oil. Slowly drizzle into peanut mixture, processing until mixture is creamy and smooth.

Rockfish:

4 (8-ounce) rockfish filets, skin on

8 slices Virginia country ham, sliced thin

Salt to taste

Pepper to taste

2 tablespoons oil, divided

Preheat oven to 375°. Prepare rockfish filets, removing any bones and seasoning skin-free side with salt and pepper. Rub baking sheet with 1 tablespoon oil. Heat remaining oil in sauté pan over high heat. Carefully place rockfish, skin-side up, in pan. Cook for about 3 minutes, until fish begins to brown. Remove filets and place skin-side down on baking sheet. Roast in oven 10 minutes, checking to make sure fish is cooked but still moist. Serve rockfish over 2 thin slices of country ham and top with pesto to taste.

Chef Patrick Evans-Hylton
Virginia Beach

Sesame Crusted Tuna with Ginger Sauce

4 (6- to 8-ounce) tuna fillets
Salt and pepper to taste
2 tablespoons olive oil
1 tablespoon white sesame seeds
1 tablespoon black sesame seeds

Pat tuna fillets dry and season with salt and pepper. Heat olive oil in skillet over medium heat. In small bowl combine sesame seeds. Press seeds onto each fillet on both sides. Return fillets to hot skillet and cook 2 minutes on each side.

Ginger Sauce:
2 tablespoons minced fresh ginger
1 large garlic clove
¼ cup soy sauce
1 tablespoon toasted sesame oil
2 tablespoons white wine or sherry
2 tablespoons rice vinegar
4 scallions, white and tender green parts, thinly sliced (divided)
2 tablespoons minced fresh mint and whole leaves for garnish

Combine all ingredients, reserving ¼ part scallions for garnish. Serve over fish.

Roya Gharavi
Gourmet Pantry & Cooking School
Blacksburg Fork and Cork

Lemon Pepper Fish

2 pounds white fish
½ cup white wine (best with MountainRose Vineyard's
    Splashdam wine)
Lemon pepper to taste
Dill weed to taste
4 tablespoons butter

Wash and pat dry fish; set aside. Combine wine with lemon pepper and dill weed. Add fish and wine mixture to plastic bag and marinate 1 hour. Melt butter in skillet over medium-high heat; add fish. Cook until fish looks opaque and turn. Cook second side until fish flakes easily with fork. Serve immediately.

Mountain Rose Vineyard • www.mountainrosevineyard.com
Wise County Famous Fall Fling

New River

Giles County is graced by 37 miles of the majestic New River, the world's second oldest waterway and one of only two that flow north. Much of the river's course is lined with steep cliffs and rock outcrops making it one of the most scenic rivers in Virginia.

Scallops Amaretto

1 medium shallot, minced	4 ounces amaretto
2 cups quartered mushrooms	2 cups heavy cream
2 tablespoons butter	1 tablespoon cornstarch
3 pounds fresh scallops	1 tablespoon water
(20/30 count)	Salt and white pepper to taste

Sauté shallots and mushrooms in butter for 2 minutes. Add scallops and cook 3 minutes. Remove scallops and set aside. Add amaretto to mushrooms and cook until most liquid is evaporated. Add heavy cream and bring to boil, being careful to not boil over. Boil until liquid is reduced by ⅓. Mix cornstarch and water and add to sauce. When thickened, add scallops and reduce heat. Season with salt and white pepper. Serve with rice pasta.

Chef Michael Porterfield, Executive Chef
Mountain Lake Conservancy & Hotel

Mountain Lake Conservancy & Hotel

115 Hotel Circle • Pembroke
540-626-7121
www.mountainlakehotel.com

Historic Mountain Lake Conservancy & Hotel is Southwestern Virginia's most comfortable family adventure getaway location. With a visit to this pristine 2,600-acre mountaintop property, guests will enjoy activities, entertainment, and adventure, or they may choose to simply relax and let the clean mountain air fill their lungs and cleanse their spirit.

Some may recognize the property from "Dirty Dancing." The hit movie was filmed in part at Mountain Lake (Kellerman's) in 1986. If you are a fan, or simply enjoy a fun and lively time, check out one of Mountain Lake's "Dirty Dancing" weekends.

In the tradition of the "Grand Southern Hotel," the warm and attentive staff at Mountain Lake ensures visits are comfortable and rewarding. Plan your visit today so that you, too, can enjoy Mountain Lake Conservancy & Hotel where guests can "Do it all, or do nothing at all."

Delicious Bay Scallops

2 pounds scallops
2 tablespoons olive oil
2 tablespoons butter
1 cup chopped mushrooms
1 small onion, chopped
Flour

¾ cup white cooking wine
¼ teaspoon curry
Salt and pepper to taste
¼ teaspoon celery salt
¾ cup sour cream

Wash scallops and set aside. In large pan, combine butter and oil over medium heat. Sauté mushrooms and onions until tender. Coat scallops thinly with flour and place in pan, browning on all sides. Add wine, curry, salt, pepper and celery salt. Cover and lower heat; simmer 10 minutes. Place scallops on serving plate; set aside. Add sour cream to pan, mixing well just to boiling point. Pour over scallops. Serve immediately.

Virginia Highlands Festival

Smothered Andouille Sausage and Shrimp with Creamy Stone Ground Grits

3 tablespoons butter
3 tablespoons flour
1 cup chopped onions
½ cup chopped green bell peppers
½ cup chopped celery
Salt to taste
Cayenne pepper to taste
1 pound Andouille sausage, sliced ¼-inch thick
1½ pounds medium shrimp, peeled and deveined
3 cups water
¼ cup chopped green onions
Creamy Stone Ground Grits (see page 112)

Melt butter in saucepan over medium heat. Stir in flour and cook 4 to 6 minutes, stirring constantly, making a medium brown roux. Add onions, peppers, celery, salt and cayenne pepper. Cook 8 minutes or until vegetables are wilted. Add sausage and cook 2 minutes. Season shrimp with salt and cayenne pepper; add to roux. Add water and simmer 8 to 10 minutes (mixture will coat back of spoon). Remove from heat and stir in green onions. Serve over Creamy Stone Ground Grits.

Virginia Highlands Festival

Grilled Shrimp

2 pounds large shrimp	1 teaspoon salt
1 cup olive oil	1 teaspoon pepper
½ cup lemon juice	3 tablespoons brown sugar
½ cup lime juice	2 tablespoons soy sauce
2 tablespoons French dressing	1 cup chopped green onion

Peel, wash and devein shrimp; set aside. Combine oil, lemon juice, French dressing, salt, pepper, brown sugar, soy sauce and green onion. Add shrimp to mixture and marinate 2 hours. Remove and place in grill basket. Reserve marinade. Cook over medium hot coals 10 minutes, turning often. Use reserved marinade as dipping sauce.

The Island House Restaurant

17 Atlantic Avenue • Wachapreague
757-787-4242
www.wachapreague.com

Tucked behind pristine barrier beach islands on the seaside of Virginia's Eastern Shore is the little town of Wachapreague. Fishing of all types, unfettered beaches, hunting and bird-watching are just a few of the attractions of this quaint town.

A popular restaurant destination in Wachapreague is The Island House Restaurant overlooking Wachapreague Harbor. Designed after the old Parramore Island Life Saving Station, which was built in the 1800s, The Island House Restaurant is a 200 seat fine dining establishment. In addition to the view from the dining room, guests may also climb the spiral staircase to reach the lookout tower for a spectacular panoramic view of the barrier islands.

Fresh local clams, oysters, certified Angus beef burgers and steaks are a few of their specialties. Call for reservations and visit the website for more information on Wachapreague.

Kelly's Grilled Shrimp

2 pounds jumbo shrimp, peeled and deveined
¼ cup vegetable oil
3 tablespoons fresh lemon juice
1 bunch green onions, finely chopped
¼ cup finely chopped parsley
3 garlic cloves, finely chopped
1 teaspoon dried basil
1 teaspoon dry mustard
1 teaspoon sea salt

Place raw shrimp in glass bowl or heavy freezer bag. Combine remaining ingredients and mix well. Pour over shrimp. Cover or close bag and refrigerate 3 to 4 hours. Grill over hot coals for 5 to 7 minutes, turning half way thru cooking. Be careful not to overcook. Shrimp are done when they turn pink.

Kelly Weinberg Foundation
The Bodacious Bazaar & Art Festival

Clams Provencal

12 clams
1 cup cornmeal
1 tablespoon extra virgin olive oil
2 garlic cloves, minced
Pinch hot pepper flakes
1 teaspoon Italian seasoning

⅓ cup white wine
⅓ cup clam juice
Pinch fresh thyme
½ cup diced tomatoes
Pinch Italian parsley

Wash and purge clams in water and cornmeal for 1 hour. Scrub well. Heat oil in saucepan, add garlic, hot pepper flakes and Italian seasoning. Sauté 3 to 4 minutes. Add wine, clam juice, thyme and tomatoes. Add clams, cover and bring to boil. As clams open, pull and place in serving bowl. When all clams are out, continuing cooking liquid to desired consistency. Pour over clams and sprinkle with parsley. Serve with bread or over pasta.

Shelly Cusmina
Bay Creek Resort and Club

The Atlantic waters off the Virginia Coast offer world-class deep-sea fishing.

thinkstockphotos.com

Chincoteague Clam Pot Pie

3 quarts water
1 large onion, chopped
3 large potatoes, cubed
2 pints shucked clams, chopped
   (reserve liquid)

1 (12-ounce) package Anne's
   dumplings
Flour
4 to 5 tablespoons bacon grease
Salt and pepper to taste

Bring water to a boil. Add onion and potatoes; boil 10 minutes. Add clams and juice, boil for an additional 5 minutes. Gradually add dumplings, alternating with a pinch of flour to keep dumplings from sticking. Stir constantly, adding water as needed. Add bacon grease and stir until completely incorporated, about 3 minutes. Salt and pepper to taste.

Donna Mason
Chincoteague Island Chamber of Commerce

Deviled Crab Casserole

1 pound crabmeat
1 tablespoon Worcestershire sauce
3 tablespoons canned milk
1 tablespoon prepared mustard
1 cup breadcrumbs
¼ cup butter, melted

Mix all ingredients together and place in baking dish. Combine breadcrumbs and butter, spread evenly on top. Bake at 350° until crumbs brown.

Stratford Hall

Bay View Inn Crab Omelette

½ cup cream of crab soup

3 eggs, beaten

1 to 2 pinches McCormick's
   Mediterranean Spiced Sea Salt

¼ teaspoon fresh cracked McCormick's
   Peppercorn Medley

1 tablespoon butter

1 tablespoon chopped red onion

1 tablespoon chopped yellow bell pepper

1 tablespoon shredded Mozzarella cheese

⅛ cup fresh crabmeat

1 tablespoon shredded Mexican blend
   cheese

Old Bay Seasoning to taste

1 fully cooked crab claw, for garnish,
   optional

In saucepan, heat crab soup. Blend 3 tablespoons crab soup with eggs. Add sea salt and peppercorn medley. Preheat flat griddle to 275°. Coat with butter. Evenly spread eggs onto griddle about ¹⁄₁₆-inch thick. Once eggs begin to turn white evenly spread 3 tablespoons crab soup over eggs. Add onion, yellow bell pepper and Mozzarella cheese. Add 4 to 5 lumps crabmeat and continue cooking. Fold omelette several times until about 2-inches wide. Sprinkle Mexican blend cheese on top. Spoon remaining crab soup over omelette. Season with Old Bay Seasoning. Garnish with cooked crab claw. Serve hot.

Bay View Inn Bed & Breakfast

Crab Cakes

½ cup rice flour
½ teaspoon seafood seasoning
½ teaspoon dried basil
½ teaspoon lemon pepper

½ cup mayonnaise
½ teaspoon Italian season
2½ pounds crabmeat
Cornmeal

Whisk together flour, seafood seasoning, basil, lemon pepper, mayonnaise and Italian seasoning in mixing bowl. Add crabmeat and toss by hand until coated. Cover and refrigerate 45 minutes. Make patties and coat in cornmeal before cooking. Cook on high heat until golden brown

Chef Shaun Phillips
The Palisades Restaurant

Virginia Beach

Crab Extraordinaire

6 tablespoons butter	4 tablespoons dry vermouth
2 tablespoons flour	Salt and pepper to taste
1½ cups light cream	4 drops hot sauce
3 egg yolks, beaten	2 tablespoons chopped parsley
1 (5-ounce) can crabmeat, drained	Paprika

Melt butter in skillet over medium heat. Add flour, stirring constantly. Add cream slowly, stirring until thickened. Add 2 teaspoons cream mixture to eggs, stir; add eggs to pan. Stir constantly until thickened. Add crabmeat, vermouth, salt, pepper, hot sauce and parsley; mix well. Continue to cook until thoroughly heated. Sprinkle with paprika and serve over toast.

Four Sails Resort

Four Sails Resort

3301 Atlantic Avenue • Virginia Beach
800-227-4213 • 757-491-8100 • www.foursails.com

The Four Sails Resort is an ocean front resort on famed Virginia Beach. Located at the exclusive north end of the oceanfront, Four Sails Resort provides the comfort of home with exceptional views, endless recreational possibilities, and a fantastic indoor pool—all right on the white sand beach. Two-bedroom and penthouse units are available, with kitchens, private balconies and large whirlpool baths. Guests have access to an exercise room, sauna and sun deck. Call or visit their website for information and reservations.

Desserts & Other Sweets

Ginger Cookies

3 sticks butter, softened
½ cup dark molasses
2 cups sugar
2 eggs
4 cups flour

4 teaspoons baking soda
2 teaspoons cinnamon
1 teaspoon ginger
1 teaspoon cloves
Sugar to taste

Cream together butter, molasses, sugar and eggs. Add flour, baking soda, cinnamon, ginger and cloves; mix well. Refrigerate dough 4 hours. Make into small balls and roll in sugar. Bake at 350° for 8 to 10 minutes or until firm and light brown.

Stratford Hall

Stratford Hall

483 Great House Road • Stratford
804-493-8038 • www.stratfordhall.org

Built by Thomas Lee in the 1730s, Stratford Hall is one of the great houses of American history. Four generations of the Lee family passed through its doors: Richard Henry Lee and Francis Lightfoot Lee, the only two brothers to sign the Declaration of Independence, and Revolutionary War hero "Light Horse Harry" Lee and his son, Civil War General Robert E. Lee. General Lee was born at Stratford in 1807.

Set on 1,900 acres on the Potomac River in Westmoreland County, Stratford Hall today offers a tranquil setting with many leisure activities for the whole family. Guests may tour the Visitor Center and its galleries, take a tour of the Great House, or walk the expansive grounds and view the beautiful gardens. In addition to the historical tours, visitors can take advantage of the many nature trails available for hiking or hunt for sharks teeth on the beach. Be sure to visit the website. Stratford Hall hosts many events throughout the year.

Mom's Old-Fashioned Molasses Cake

½ teaspoon salt
1¼ teaspoons ground cinnamon
½ teaspoon ground cloves
1 teaspoon ground ginger
1 teaspoon baking soda
½ cup shortening

½ cup packed brown sugar
1 cup molasses
2 eggs
2½ cups cake flour
1 cup brewed coffee

Preheat oven to 350°. Sift together salt, cinnamon, cloves, ginger, flour and baking soda. In a separate bowl, combine shortening and sugar, beating with an electric mixer. Add molasses and eggs; cream well. Add dry mixture gradually. Stir in coffee. Pour into greased and floured sheet pan and bake 30 minutes. Cool completely.

Black Walnut and Brown Sugar Cake

3 sticks butter, softened
1 (16-ounce) box light brown sugar
1 cup white sugar
5 eggs
3 cups flour

½ teaspoon baking powder
1 cup milk
1 tablespoon vanilla extract
1 cup black walnuts

Preheat oven to 325°. Cream together butter and sugars. Add eggs 1 at a time. In separate bowl, mix flour and baking powder. Alternately add milk and dry mixture to batter. Add vanilla and nuts. Pour into greased and floured tube pan. Bake 1½ hours.

Uncle Gene
Culpeper Air Fest

Dream Coffee Cake

1 box yellow cake mix
4 eggs
1 cup oil
1 cup sour cream

¾ cup sugar
1¾ cups chopped nuts
1½ teaspoons cinnamon

Preheat oven to 350°. Combine cake mix, eggs, oil and sour cream; mix well. In separate bowl, combine sugar, nuts and cinnamon. Pour ½ cake batter into bottom of 9x13-inch baking dish. Cover with ½ nut mixture. Repeat. Bake 40 minutes.

Jane
Culpeper Air Fest

Caramel Icing

2 cups light brown sugar
½ cup whipping cream
½ teaspoon vanilla extract

Combine sugar and cream in saucepan over medium-low heat. Cook until sugar is dissolved but not grainy. Add vanilla and let come to light boil until it drops in sheets from a spoon. Remove from heat and whip until stiff enough to spread on cake.

Edith Stickley
Grand Caverns

Chocolate Decadence with Chocolate Ganache

2 sticks butter	8 eggs
2 tablespoons water	2 tablespoons flour
2 cups semi-sweet chocolate chips	

Preheat oven to 425°. Prepare a 10-inch cake pan with nonstick spray and parchment paper (cut to fit bottom). Place butter and water in a 2-quart saucepan over medium heat. Bring to boil and add chocolate chips; turn off heat. Let set 4 to 5 minutes, then mix till well combined. In separate bowl, whisk eggs until double in size. Add flour gradually. Add chocolate. Pour mixture into pan. Bake 12 minutes, just till middle shakes like Jell-O. Cool and refrigerate 12 to 24 hours. Trim edges to make flat top. Flip onto cooling rack.

Chocolate Ganache:

1¼ cups heavy cream	1¼ cups semi-sweet chocolate chips

Bring cream to boil in 2-quart saucepan; remove from heat. Add chocolate chips and let stand about 4 minutes. Mix chocolate into cream till well combined. Pour over cake and smooth over to run down the sides. Refrigerate to set Ganache.

Mary Martin
Rockingham County Fair

Rockingham County Fair

August

Rockingham Fairgrounds
Harrisonburg
540-434-0005
www.rockinghamcountyfair.com

The Rockingham County Fair is Virginia's leading agricultural county fair. It was named by the Los Angeles Times as one of the Top Ten agricultural fairs in the U.S. and has been presented awards from the International Association of Fairs and Expositions on 18 occasions for its agricultural programming. The fair features livestock and poultry shows, farm crops and horticultural exhibits, as well as commercial and non-profit exhibits. Entertainment includes national music acts, tractor pulls, demolition derbies, motocross racing, and bull riding. All food and concessions are prepared by local community service organizations.

Hot Fudge Pudding Cake

1 cup buttermilk baking mix
1 cup sugar, divided
⅓ cup plus 3 tablespoons cocoa, divided
½ cup milk
1 teaspoon vanilla
1⅔ cups hot tap water

Preheat oven to 350°. In bowl, combine baking mix, ½ cup sugar and 3 tablespoons cocoa. Stir in milk and vanilla. Spread in 8-inch square pan. Sprinkle with remaining ⅓ cup cocoa and ½ cup sugar. Pour hot water on top. Do not stir. Bake 40 minutes or until top is firm. Pudding will form on bottom.

Barbara Barger
Virginia Southern Gospel Jubilee

Big Walker Lookout

Big Walker Lookout boasts spectacular views of the Appalachian Mountains. Located near the BW Country Store, visitors can climb the 100 foot Lookout Tower to enjoy a view where "Only The Birds See More."

Irish Chocolate Potato Cake

½ pound butter, softened
2 cups sugar
4 eggs, beaten
3 ounces unsweetened chocolate, melted
1 cup cold mashed potatoes
1 teaspoon cinnamon

½ teaspoon cloves
½ teaspoon allspice
2 cups flour
1 teaspoon baking soda
1 cup sour milk
1 cup chopped walnuts

Preheat oven to 350°. Cream butter and add sugar gradually, beating until light and fluffy. Add eggs and beat well. Add chocolate, potatoes and spices. Sift flour and baking soda together and add to chocolate mixture alternately with milk. Beat well. Add nuts and mix lightly. Bake in greased 10-inch tube pan about 70 minutes.

Mocha Icing:

½ cup butter
3 cups powdered sugar
1 tablespoon cocoa

Strong hot coffee
1 teaspoon vanilla

Cream butter with powdered sugar and cocoa. Add coffee for desired consistency. Add vanilla and stir well.

Mrs. Abigail Kime
BW Country Store

Mayonnaise Cake

3 cups flour
1½ cups mayonnaise
1½ cups sugar
3 teaspoons soda

6 tablespoons cocoa
1½ teaspoons vanilla
1½ cups hot water

Combine all ingredients and pour into ungreased 9x13-inch pan.
Bake at 350° for 25 to 30 minutes or until toothpick inserted in
middle comes out clean. Frost with white icing.

Sandee Burt, Moneta
Smith Mountain Lake

Smith Mountain Lake

Located in central Virginia along the Blue Ridge Mountains
540-721-1203 • www.visitsmithmountainlake.com

Smith Mountain Lake is an amazing region
covering three counties—Bedford, Franklin
and Pittsylvania. People from all walks of life,
nearby and from far away, have found Smith
Mountain Lake to be the ideal place for a short
get-away or to 'set their anchor' for a lifetime.
With a clear glistening lake covering 500
miles of shoreline, four breathtaking seasons
of color in a moderate climate, surrounded by
the Blue Ridge Mountains and central to the
metropolitan areas

of Roanoke, Lynchburg and Martinsville, what's not to love? Smith
Mountain Lake provides the perfect setting for every interest and
lifestyle, be it wall-to-wall activities or just plain quiet and relaxing.
Visit their website to view video clips and to order a free visitor guide.

Catherine's Chocolate Zucchini Cake

2½ cups flour
¼ cup unsweetened cocoa
1 teaspoon baking soda
½ teaspoon salt
½ teaspoon ground cinnamon
¼ teaspoon ground cloves
½ cup unsalted butter, softened
½ cup vegetable oil

1¾ cups sugar
2 large eggs
1 teaspoon vanilla extract
½ cup buttermilk
3 cups grated zucchini
1½ cups chocolate chips
½ cup chopped pecans

Preheat oven to 350°. Grease and flour 9x13-inch baking dish. Whisk together flour, cocoa, baking soda, salt and spices; set aside. Cream together butter, oil and sugar with electric mixer. Add eggs, vanilla and buttermilk. Beat until well blended. Add flour mixture to butter mixture, blending thoroughly. Mix in zucchini and spread into prepared dish. Sprinkle chocolate chips and nuts on top. Bake 40 to 45 minutes.

Culpeper Air Fest

Zucchini Cake

3 beaten eggs
1 cup vegetable oil
2 cups sugar
2 cups grated zucchini
3 cups flour
3 teaspoons cinnamon
½ teaspoon nutmeg

2 teaspoons baking soda
½ teaspoon baking powder
2 teaspoons vanilla
1 cup nuts
½ cup raisins
1 cup drained, crushed pineapple
½ teaspoon salt

Preheat oven to 350°. Mix first 4 ingredients together. Add flour and mix well. Add spices, baking soda, baking powder and vanilla. Stir in nuts, raisins and pineapple. Pour in greased and floured 9x13-inch pan. Bake 1 hour.

Cream Cheese Frosting:

3 ounces cream cheese, softened
1 tablespoon butter

2 cups powdered sugar
1 teaspoon vanilla

Cream together all ingredients and spread on cooled cake.

Sandee Burt, Moneta
Smith Mountain Lake

Sandra's Carrot Cake

2 cups sugar
2 cups self-rising flour
1 teaspoon cinnamon
Dash ground clove
1½ cups oil

4 eggs
1 teaspoon vanilla extract
2 cups chopped walnuts
2 to 3 cups grated carrots

Preheat oven to 350°. Grease and flour tube pan. Combine all ingredients 1 at a time, mixing well after each addition. Pour into prepared pan and bake 1 to 1½ hours.

Glaze:

4 tablespoons corn syrup
1 cup sugar

1 cup buttermilk
1 teaspoon baking soda

During the last 10 minutes bake time, mix glaze ingredients in saucepan and bring to a boil. Pour over hot cake while still in pan, allowing glaze to soak into cake. Let cool about ½ hour, turn out on cake plate. No icing needed!

The Bodacious Bazaar & Art Festival

Sweet Potato Cake

2 cups sugar
2½ cups flour
1½ cups cooked sweet potatoes
1½ cups oil
3 eggs
1½ teaspoons cinnamon

1½ teaspoons nutmeg
1½ teaspoons allspice
2 teaspoons baking powder
2 teaspoons baking soda
2 teaspoons vanilla

Preheat oven to 350°. Grease and flour 3 (8-inch) cake pans. Combine all ingredients, stirring thoroughly. Pour into pans. Bake 30 minutes. Cool on wire racks.

Icing:

1 (8-ounce) package cream cheese, softened
1 cup chopped pecans

1 stick butter
¾ box (16-ounce) powdered sugar
Milk for consistency, as needed

Mix ingredients together and spread in between layers, top and sides of cake. Refrigerate.

Jackie Erickson
Ben Lomond

Mountain Meadow Farm and Craft Market

Grandma's Pumpkin Patch Cake

2 cups sifted cake flour
1½ teaspoons baking soda
2 cups sugar
4 eggs
2 teaspoons cinnamon
½ teaspoon salt
2 teaspoons baking powder
1 cup oil
1 (16-ounce) can pumpkin

Preheat oven to 350°. Combine all ingredients and mix well. Pour batter into 2 (9-inch) baking pans. Bake 35 minutes.

Icing:

1 (8-ounce) package cream
  cheese, softened
1 stick butter, softened
1 box powdered sugar
1 teaspoon vanilla

Cream together all ingredients. Spread over cooled cake and between layers.

Sue's Pumpkin Patch
Mountain Meadow Farm

Dump Cake

1 (21-ounce) can cherry pie filling
1 (8-ounce) small can crushed
  pineapples
1 box yellow cake mix
1 package slivered almonds
1 (3½-ounce) can coconut
2 sticks butter

Combine cherry pie filling and pineapples and place into 9x13-inch pan. Sprinkle cake mix, almonds and coconut on top. Slice butter on top and bake 1 hour at 350°.

Beverly Viers
Wise County Famous Fall Fling

Apple Cake

3 cups flour
2 cups sugar
1 teaspoon baking soda
½ teaspoon salt
2 teaspoons cinnamon

1 cup oil
3 eggs
2 teaspoons vanilla extract
2 to 3 cups diced apples
1 cup chopped pecans

Preheat oven to 350°. Mix dry ingredients till well blended.
Add oil, eggs and vanilla. Fold in apples and pecans. Pour into
greased and floured sheet baking pan. Bake 1 hour.

Icing:

1 stick butter
½ cup evaporated milk

¾ cup powdered sugar
1 teaspoon vanilla extract

Mix butter, milk and sugar in saucepan and boil 1 minute over
medium-high heat. Add vanilla and stir. Spread ½ icing on cake
while in pan and let cool completely. Turn cake out and spread
remaining icing on top.

June Wilson
Richlands Fall Festival

Richlands, Virginia

Catherine's Fresh Apple Cake

3 cups flour
1 teaspoon soda
½ teaspoon salt
1 teaspoon cinnamon
3 eggs
2 cups sugar
1¼ cups oil

2 tablespoons vanilla extract
½ cup orange juice
1 cup walnuts (do not chop)
1 cup pecans (do not chop)
½ cup shredded coconut
4 cups mixed (tart/sweet) apples, thickly sliced (unpeeled)

Preheat oven to 325°. Combine flour, baking soda, salt and cinnamon. In separate bowl, beat eggs, sugar and oil. Slowly add dry mixture to wet mixture; add vanilla and orange juice. Mix well. Add walnuts, pecans and coconut. Add apples. Pour in greased tube pan and bake 1¼ to 1½ hours or until toothpick inserted in center comes out clean.

Glaze:

½ cup butter
1 cup sugar

½ cup buttermilk
½ teaspoon baking soda

In saucepan, melt butter and sugar. Add buttermilk. When warm, add baking soda and stir continuously. Mixture will foam and swell. Stir several minutes. Using fork, generously poke holes around top of cake while still warm. Pour slowly over cake, making sure all sides are covered. Immediately turn out onto dish with a slight well, topping will pool around outside.

Culpeper Air Fest

Fresh Apple Cake

2 eggs, beaten
2 cups sugar
1 cup oil
2½ cups flour
1 teaspoon salt

2 teaspoons baking soda
1 teaspoon cinnamon
4 cups raw chopped apples
1 cup chopped nuts

Preheat oven to 325°. Grease and flour 1 Bundt pan. In a medium size bowl, mix eggs, sugar and oil; let stand 20 minutes. In a separate bowl, sift together flour, salt, baking soda and cinnamon. Add dry ingredients to egg mixture; mix well. Add apples and nuts and stir thoroughly. Pour into pan and bake 1 hour or until toothpick inserted comes out clean.

Jackie Erickson
Ben Lomond

Historic sites near Ben Lomond

(See page 139 for more information on Ben Lomond.)

Bristoe Station Battlefield Heritage Park, site of Civil War encampments and the August 1862 Battle of Kettle Run and the October 1863 Battle of Bristoe Station.

Brentsville Courthouse Historic Centre consists of the original courthouse and jail which served as seat of the county government for most of the 19th century. Other buildings of note include an 1850s farm house and 1920s school house.

Rippon Lodge Historic Site is one of the oldest surviving houses in Northern Virginia, having been constructed around 1747. Originally the home of the Blackburn family, with close ties to the Washington's at Mount Vernon, Rippon Lodge is open to the public.

Old Fashioned Fresh Apple Cake

1 cup vegetable oil
2 eggs
2 cups sugar
2½ cups plain flour
1 teaspoon salt
1 teaspoon baking soda

1 teaspoon baking powder
1 teaspoon cinnamon
1 cup chopped pecans
3 cups chopped tart cooking apples
1 (6-ounce) bag butterscotch chips

In large bowl, combine oil, eggs and sugar. In a separate bowl, sift together flour, salt, soda, baking powder and cinnamon. Add to first mixture. Stir in chopped pecans and apples. Mix well. Spread mixture into a greased 9x13-inch baking pan. Distribute butterscotch chips on top. Bake at 350° for 55 to 60 minutes. Cool and cut into squares. For best results, bake 1 day before serving.

Kate Hibbits
Wise County Famous Fall Fling

Michelle's Cherry Ice Box Cake

1 (12-ounce) container Cool Whip,
    thawed
1 large box instant vanilla pudding

2 cups milk
1 box graham crackers
2 (21-ounce) cans cherry pie filling

In large bowl, combine Cool Whip and pudding; mix well. Gradually add milk. Once completely mixed, let stand 5 minutes. It will thicken slightly. Layer graham crackers in 9x13-inch pan and top with ½ pudding mixture. Place another graham cracker layer on top, and pour remaining pudding mixture. Apply final graham cracker layer on top and pour both cans cherry pie filling on top. Cover and chill overnight before serving.

Edinburg Mill

Cherry Wheat Beer Cake

¾ cup maraschino cherries, divided
2 cups flour, sifted
2 teaspoons baking powder
¼ teaspoon salt
4 eggs, at room temperature

2 cups sugar
2 teaspoons vanilla extract
1 cup Sam Adams Cherry Wheat beer
2 tablespoons butter, melted

Preheat oven to 375°. Grease and flour Bundt cake pan. Remove stems and halve 16 cherries lengthwise and arrange in bottom and up sides of small channels in Bundt pan. There should be 8 evenly-spaced rows in spokes going outward from center tube. Chop remaining cherries to make ¼ cup, squeeze dry in paper towels, and set aside. In medium bowl, whisk together flour, baking powder and salt. Set aside. In large bowl, beat eggs until thick and light in color, about 3 to 5 minutes. Beat in sugar ¼ cup at a time until combined. Add vanilla extract. Using large spatula, fold flour mixture into sugar mixture. In saucepan, heat 1 cup beer until bubbles begin to rise around edge. Add warm beer and butter to batter, stirring gently to combine. Pour batter into prepared pan, being careful not to dislodge cherries (batter will appear thin). Bake 30 minutes. Do not over-bake. Cool on rack for 10 minutes, and loosen cake around inner and outer edges of pan. Invert onto large platter and cool.

Glaze:

2 tablespoons Sam Adams Cherry
    Wheat beer

1 cup powdered sugar

Whisk together beer and powdered sugar until smooth. Drizzle over cake.

Chef Randall Spencer
Blue Ridge Mountain Catering
Blacksburg Fork and Cork

Blackberry Cake

1 cup butter, softened
3 cups sugar
4 eggs
2 cups canned blackberries
4 cups flour

2 teaspoons allspice
1 teaspoon cloves
4 teaspoons baking powder
½ cup buttermilk

Cream together butter and sugar. Add eggs 1 at a time, beating after each. Add blackberries. In a separate bowl, combine flour, allspice, cloves and baking powder. Gradually add to blackberry mixture with buttermilk. Pour into cake pans and bake at 350° for 30 minutes.

Icing:

2½ cups sugar
½ cup light corn syrup
½ cup water

3 egg whites
1 teaspoon vanilla

In a saucepan, bring sugar, syrup and water to soft boil. Beat egg whites until stiff. Pour syrup into egg whites and gradually beat. Add vanilla and beat until fluffy. Spread on cooled cake.

Virginia Highlands Festival

Virginia Highlands Festival

July – August

Held throughout the Historic Downtown area
Northeast Abingdon
276-623-5266
www.vahighlandsfestival.org

The Virginia Highlands Festival has been in existence for more than sixty years. Robert Porterfield, founder of the Barter Theatre, started the Festival in 1949 as a one-week festival to showcase Appalachian arts and crafts. The festival has now grown into a variety of venues. Every year hundreds of volunteers work to create exciting new "impressions" of the festival for visitors to enjoy. It is highlighted by juried arts and crafts, fine arts, performing arts, and an award winning antiques market. Other events are planned each year to entice shoppers, artists, youth, conservationists, adventurers, and educators to the mountains of Southwest Virginia to see the jewels of Appalachia. Visitors can join in the concurrent events that take place, such as theatrical readings at the Barter, the making of cigar box guitars, and the touring of cultural museums.

Snow Ball Cake

2 envelopes unflavored gelatin
4 teaspoons cold water
1 cup boiling water
1 cup sugar
1 package frozen coconut,
  divided
3 teaspoons lemon juice
1 large package frozen
  strawberries
2 large containers Cool Whip
1 prepared angel food cake,
  cubed

Soften gelatin in 4 teaspoons cold water. Add boiling water and
stir until well dissolved. Add sugar, ⅓ package coconut, lemon
juice and strawberries. Allow to stand 15 minutes to thicken.
Add 1 container Cool Whip. Line deep dish with ½ cake cubes.
Spread fruit mixture atop cake. Top cake with remaining carton
Cool Whip. Sprinkle with remaining coconut. Chill 4 hours.

Vickie Slater
Virginia Southern Gospel Jubilee

Herbs Galore & More

Strawberries with Pineapple Sage Shortcake

This recipe is a variation of the traditional strawberry shortcake. Pineapple sage has a nice, light fruity flavor which complements strawberries.

Strawberry Filling:
2 cups sliced strawberries
¼ cup sugar
1 tablespoon minced fresh pineapple sage

In a small bowl, combine strawberries, sugar and pineapple sage; set aside.

Pineapple Sage Shortcake:
2 cups all-purpose flour
2 tablespoons baking powder
6 tablespoons butter, chilled
1 cup milk or plain soy milk
2 tablespoons minced fresh pineapple sage
⅓ cup sugar
Whipped cream, for garnish

Preheat oven to 425°. Sift together flour and baking powder. Cut butter into dry ingredients using a pastry knife or 2 knives until dough has texture of coarse cornmeal. Stir in milk, pineapple sage and sugar; mix well. Drop by ⅓-cup portions onto a greased baking sheet. Bake 18 to 20 minutes until lightly browned on bottom. Let cool to room temperature and cut each cake in half lengthwise. Top each half with strawberry filling and whipped cream.

Nicole Schermerhorn, owner, A Thyme to Plant Herb Farm
Herbs Galore & More at Maymont

Easy Peach Cake

2 cups coarsely chopped fresh
    peaches (frozen can be used as
    a substitute)
2 tablespoons chopped pecans
1 tablespoon butter, melted

1 package yellow cake mix, plus
    ingredients to prepare per
    package directions
3 eggs
1 teaspoon ground cinnamon

Preheat oven to 375°. Place peaches and pecans in bottom of greased 8-inch square baking pan. Drizzle butter over peaches. Prepare cake mix according to package directions using 3 eggs and adding cinnamon. Spoon batter over peaches. Bake 30 to 40 minutes or until golden brown. Invert pan. Cool 5 minutes before removing. May be served warm or cold.

Amanda Wingfield, Patrick County Extension Office
Virginia State Peach Festival

Virginia State Peach Festival

Wedding Cake

This is a very dense cake. Served at our 18th Century Weddings.

½ cup butter, plus more for pan
½ cup sugar
2 tablespoons brandy (may substitute with vanilla extract)
2 tablespoons sherry (may substitute with orange or pineapple juice)
4 eggs
1 cup currants, soaked in hot water (may substitute with raisins)

2 cups wheat flour
½ teaspoon ginger
½ teaspoon mace
½ teaspoon cloves
½ teaspoon cinnamon
½ teaspoon nutmeg
¾ cup sliced almonds
Candied citron, orange and lemon to taste, optional

Preheat oven to 350°. Grease 9-inch round pan with butter. Combine butter and sugar until well blended. Slowly add brandy, sherry, eggs and currants. In a separate bowl, mix flour, ginger, mace, cloves, cinnamon, nutmeg, almonds and candied citrons. Slowly add flour mixture into butter mixture, stirring until well blended. Bake 45 minutes to 1 hour or until knife inserted in center comes out clean.

Claude Moore Colonial Farm

Heavenly Delite

1 box yellow cake mix
1 (15-ounce) can crushed pineapple, drained
1 large box vanilla pudding mix
1 (8-ounce) package cream cheese, softened
1 (8-ounce) container Cool Whip

Bake cake according to package directions. Let cool. Poke holes in cake with fork. Spread pineapple over cake. Prepare pudding according to package directions. Add cream cheese to pudding; blend well. Spread atop pineapple. Top with Cool Whip

Tressia Boyd
Richlands Fall Festival

Hatchetmeg's Homemade Pirate Rum Cake

1 cup chopped pecans
2 sticks butter, softened
½ cup canola oil
4 eggs
1 cup buttermilk
½ cup spiced rum
½ cup water
1 tablespoon pure vanilla extract

2 cups packed light brown sugar
3 cups flour
1 teaspoon baking soda
1 teaspoon baking powder
1 cup golden macerated raisins
  (soaked in water 30 minutes to
  overnight)

Preheat oven to 325°. Grease and flour Bundt pan. Evenly cover bottom of pan with chopped pecans. Add any remaining pecans to cake batter. In large mixing bowl, blend butter and oil on low speed with electric mixer. Add eggs and buttermilk; continue beating on low speed. Add rum, water and vanilla, and increase to medium speed. Slowly add sugar. Next sift together flour, baking soda and baking powder. Add flour mixture gradually and beat until smooth, about 2 minutes. Drain raisins and add to batter using a spoon to mix. Batter should pour freely. If too thick, add rum to thin. Pour into pan slowly, making sure pecans do not move. Bake 45 to 50 minutes. Let cool.

Glaze:

4 tablespoons butter
¼ cup water
1 cup brown sugar

½ cup spiced rum
1 tablespoon real vanilla extract

In medium saucepan, combine butter, water and sugar. Cook over high heat to boil. Continue cooking 2 minutes, stirring constantly. Glaze should have the consistency of simple syrup. Remove from heat. Stir in rum and vanilla. Place serving tray upside down over cake and invert cake. Carefully poke holes around top and sides of cake. Slowly spoon glaze over top. The cake acts as a sponge and pulls the glaze in. There will still a good bit glaze in bottom of serving tray. Do not remove it, as this will be absorbed. Cake tastes best if made a day or 2 in advance.

Susan Lemieux-Cortez, a.k.a. Hatchetmeg,
Hearty member of Blackbeard's Crew
Blackbeard Pirate Festival

Blackbeard Pirate Festival

June

**Mill Point Park,
Downtown Hampton and
Hampton Waterfront
757-727-0900
www.blackbeardfestival.com**

Every June, roughly 50,000 seafaring attendees, as well as Blackbeard and his crew, invade downtown Hampton during the annual Blackbeard Pirate Festival. Visitors can interact with Blackbeard (personified by first-person interpreter Ben Cherry) and more than 100 other authentically costumed pirate re-enactors as they run rampant on the streets of America's oldest continuous English-speaking settlement. Living history and family fun go hand-in-hand as Hampton reenacts and celebrates the demise of Blackbeard, one of the fiercest pirates ever known. This 1700's pirate adventure is complete with live entertainment, pirate encampments, children's activities, sea battles, fireworks, and more.

White Oak Lavender Farm

Lavender Pound Cake

1 cup butter, softened
2 cups sugar
2 teaspoons culinary lavender
   buds
2 teaspoons vanilla
4 eggs
1½ cups flour
1½ cups cake flour
1 teaspoon salt
½ teaspoon baking powder
½ teaspoon baking soda
1 cup buttermilk

Preheat oven to 350°. Cream together butter, sugar and lavender buds. Add vanilla and eggs. Sift flours together with salt, baking powder and baking soda. Add to creamed mixture alternating with buttermilk, starting and ending with dry ingredients. Pour in greased Bundt pan and bake 50 minutes. Cool and remove from pan.

Tip: Before removing cake from pan, poke holes in hot cake and pour Lavender Butter Sauce (see page 74) on top.

White Oak Lavender Farm

Apricot Pound Cake

1 cup butter
3 cups sugar
6 eggs
½ teaspoon rum extract
1 teaspoon orange extract
½ teaspoon lemon extract
¼ teaspoon almond extract

1 teaspoon vanilla extract
1 teaspoon butter extract
3 cups sifted flour
¼ teaspoon baking soda
½ teaspoon salt
1 cup sour cream
½ cup apricot nectar

Cream butter and sugar until light and fluffy. Add eggs, 1 at a time, beating well after each. Add rum, orange, lemon, almond, vanilla and butter extracts. In a separate bowl, combine flour, baking soda and salt; set aside. In another bowl, combine sour cream and apricot nectar; mix well. Blend small portions flour mixture into butter mixture alternately with sour cream mixture. Once well blended, beat at medium speed 2 minutes. Pour into greased and floured 10-inch tube pan. Bake at 325° for 1½ hours. This cake needs the full amount of baking time, otherwise it will appear done on top and still not be done inside. If necessary, place foil loosely over the top during last part of baking to prevent too much browning. Allow to cool in pan 10 minutes. Invert onto plate and cool completely before serving.

Rita Longworth
Wise County Famous Fall Fling

3 ... 2 ... 1 - Cake!

This is perfect for those of us with just one or two in the house with no need to make a huge cake. This way you can make 1, 2, 3 or as many as you need. These individual little cakes are amazing and ready to eat in one minute! They are perfect for whenever you feel like a treat or need a quick dessert. Genius idea!

1 box Angel Food cake mix
1 box cake mix, any flavor
Water

In Ziploc bag, combine cake mixes and mix well. For each individual cake serving, us 3 tablespoons cake mix combination and mix it with 2 tablespoons water in a small microwave-safe container. Microwave on high 1 minute and you have your own instant individual little cake! Keep remaining dry cake mixture stored in Ziploc bag and use whenever you feel like a treat! You can top each cake with a dollop of fat free whipped topping and/or fresh fruit.

Recipe Reminder:

This recipe is called 3 ... 2 ... 1 - Cake! because all you need to remember is: 3 tablespoons mix, 2 tablespoons water, 1 minute in the microwave!

Variations:

Try various flavors of cake mix, carrot, red velvet, pineapple, orange, lemon, etc. Just remember, 1 of the mixes has to be Angel Food cake mix. The flavor possibilities are endless.

Hillsville Downtown Celebration Series

Gray Ghost Miniature Cheesecakes

1 box vanilla wafers, crushed
1 box (100 mini-size) baking cups
4 eggs
4 (8-ounce) packages cream cheese, softened
1 cup sugar
1 teaspoon vanilla
Raspberries, blueberries or blackberries, optional

Place 1 teaspoon vanilla wafer crumbs in each mini-size baking cup. Beat eggs. Add cream cheese, sugar and vanilla; beat well. Put about 1 tablespoon batter into each cup. Bake 12 minutes at 350°. When cooled, top with fresh fruit (optional).

Cheryl Kellert
Gray Ghost Vineyards

Gray Ghost Vineyards

14706 Lee Highway • Amissville
540-937-4869 • www.grayghostvineyards.com

Family owned and operated, Gray Ghost prides itself in using age-old winemaking methods combined with advanced technology to produce internationally acclaimed wines while preserving Virginia's rich history. Gray Ghost focuses on gentle handling from the fruit to the wine to ensure the highest quality product, resulting in over 100 medals awarded each year.

A visit to Gray Ghost offers a knowledgeable staff, southern hospitality, beautiful picnic grounds and spacious indoor facilities. Visitors should ask about Gray Ghost's famous winery events, entertaining tours and most popular volunteer harvest program.

Strawberry Pie

1 (8-inch) pie shell, baked
1 cup sugar
4 cups sliced strawberries

1 to 2 cups water
4 tablespoons cornstarch
1 tablespoon lemon juice

Combine sugar and strawberries. Let stand 2 hours, covered. Drain off juice from berries and add enough water to make 1¾ cups berry juice. Blend ¼ cup berry juice with cornstarch to form smooth paste. Put berry paste in double boiler, add remaining berry juice and cook over medium heat, stirring constantly, until berry juice boils. Reduce heat, cover and cook 12 minutes, stirring several times. Remove from heat, add lemon juice and strawberries.

Cool 10 minutes and then pour into cool pie shell. Allow to sit 1 hour before serving.

Shirley Cassidy
Wise County Famous Fall Fling

Virginia Beach

Lemon Chiffon Pie

4 eggs, separated
¾ cup sugar, divided
½ cup lemon juice
¼ teaspoon salt
¼ cup cold water

1 tablespoon (one envelope)
  plain gelatin
1 (9-inch) baked pie crust
Cool whip

Beat egg yolks. Combine with ½ cup sugar, lemon juice and salt. Cook in double-boiler until thick, stirring constantly. In cold water, dissolve gelatin; add to egg mixture. Cool until partially set. In separate bowl, beat egg whites and gradually add remaining sugar. Fold into cooled mixture. Pour into baked pie shell. Chill until firm. Top with Cool Whip before serving.

Occoquan Craft Fair

Occoquan Craft Fair
September

Occoquan's Historic District
703-491-2168
www.occoquancraftshow.com

Great music, big fun and fantastic crafts are the order of the day at the annual Occoquan Craft Fair. The fair has been going strong for over two decades, and continues to grow each year. Over 25,000 people flood into the charming river town to enjoy a weekend of shopping and food in a terrific atmosphere of friendship and

Bryan Reese

fun. With 200 to 300 craft vendors and merchants each year, the Occoquan Craft Fair promises a one-of-a-kind discovery experience. Call or visit the website for specific dates and times, as well as parking and commuting instructions.

Grandma's Apple Pie

This apple pie is incredibly delicious hot with vanilla ice cream or a slice of Cheddar cheese (an old Yankee touch).

6 cups peeled, sliced apples (Golden Delicious, Jonathan or
    Granny Smith)
1 tablespoon fresh lemon juice
½ cup sugar
½ cup firmly packed brown sugar
2 tablespoons all-purpose flour
½ teaspoon cinnamon
¼ teaspoon ground nutmeg
2 (9-inch) pie crusts
2 tablespoons butter

Preheat oven to 450°. Toss together apples and lemon juice in mixing bowl. Combine sugar, brown sugar, flour, cinnamon and nutmeg; mix well. Pour sugar mixture over apples and stir to coat. Spoon filling into 1 pie crust and dot with butter. Place 2nd pie crust over top, trimming off excess. Fold edges under to seal and flute rim. Cut slits into top pastry to allow steam to escape. Bake 15 minutes at 450°. Reduce heat to 350° and bake 45 minutes.

Crossing at the Dan

Pineapple Chess Pie

5 eggs
1 teaspoon vanilla
2 cups sugar
1 stick melted butter
1 cup grated coconut

1 (8-ounce) can crushed
  pineapple, drained
¼ teaspoon salt
2 (8-inch) unbaked pie shells

Preheat oven to 325°. Mix all ingredients together and pour into pie shells. Bake 50 minutes. Serve each slice with dollop of whipped cream and sprig of pineapple mint.

Trail of the Lonesome Pine

Trail of the Lonesome Pine

Performances held July and August on Thursday thru Saturday

276-523-1235 • www.trailofthelonesomepine.com

Big Stone Gap is a "little town with a big story." Visit their outdoor drama, Trail of the Lonesome Pine, one of the oldest in the US. It's a tender love story intermingled with folk music, feuding and a hanging of the "bad guys." While there, visit the John Fox Jr. Museum and June Tolliver Folk Art Center, both Virginia & National Historic Landmarks, where guests can purchase the museum cookbook *Dining 'Neath the Pine*. Add the Harry Meador Coal Museum and the Lonesome Pine School & Heritage Center for a great weekend of culture and discovery.

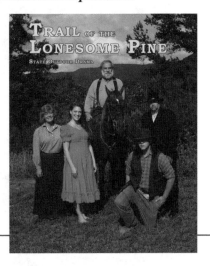

Mountain Berry Pie

1 cup sugar
¼ teaspoon salt
¼ cup cornstarch
½ teaspoon cinnamon
1 cup blueberries
1½ cup raspberries,
   blackberries or mixed berries

1 cup strawberries
½ cup water
2 tablespoons lemon juice
2 (9-inch) pie pastries
2 tablespoons butter or
   margarine

Combine sugar, salt, cornstarch and cinnamon in saucepan. Stir in berries. Add water and lemon juice. Cook over medium heat to boiling point. Pour into pie shell. Dot with butter. Top with pie pastry and cut slits in top. Brush with milk and sprinkle with sugar. Bake at 350° for 45 minutes or until crust is golden.

Dee Kime
BW Country Store

Buckland Farm Market

Nanny's Family Pie

1 cup sugar
1¼ cups flour
2 teaspoons baking powder
1 cup milk

1 stick butter, melted
2 to 3 cups fresh fruit with juice,
 sliced (may substitute canned
 pie filling)

Preheat oven to 350°. Combine sugar, flour, baking powder and milk; mix well. Pour butter into 9x13-inch glass baking dish. Pour batter into middle of melted butter. Do not stir. Pour fruit with juice over batter. Do not stir. Bake until bubbly and golden brown. Serve hot with ice cream or heavy whipping cream on top.

The Bodacious Bazaar & Art Festival

Jeff's Chocolate Cream Cheese Pie

I have been a dairy farmer's wife for 30 years, and when Jeff and I were dating I soon learned he loved chocolate pie. His grandmother spoiled him every chance she could and made the most delicious chocolate pie with a flaky soft crust that could not be duplicated. But wanting to try to something special and not having a lot of experience in the kitchen... (growing up on the farm, I avoided the kitchen and helped outside as much as possible)... I sought to make him a chocolate pie he would love. I found a winner – so easy, it's hard to mess up – and Jeff found a new favorite chocolate pie. Sorry Grandma!

¾ (8-ounce) package cream cheese, softened (6 ounces)
2 tablespoons powdered sugar
2 cups milk, divided

1 (12-ounce) carton whipped topping, divided
2 (9-inch) graham cracker crusts
2 large packages chocolate pudding mix

With electric mixer, combine cream cheese, powdered sugar, 2 tablespoons milk and ½ container whipped topping. Mix until smooth. Spoon mixture evenly in pie shells. Mix instant pudding according to directions (using remaining milk) and pour over cream cheese layer. Refrigerate 30 minutes and top with remaining whipped topping.

Patty Leonard
Cows - N - Corn

Date Macaroon Pie

12 saltines, crushed fine
1 cup sugar
12 dates, diced
½ cup chopped pecans
1 teaspoon almond extract
3 egg whites, stiffly beaten

Preheat oven to 350°. Combine saltines, sugar, dates, pecans and almond extract; mix well. Fold in egg whites. Pour in greased pie dish. Bake 10 minutes.

Stratford Hall

Coconut Pecan Pie

1 stick butter, melted
2 eggs, beaten
1 cup sugar
2 teaspoons flour
½ cup pecans, broken into pieces
¾ cup coconut
1 teaspoon white vinegar
1 teaspoon vanilla extract
1 unbaked 9-inch regular pie shell

Combine butter, eggs, sugar and flour. Add pecans, coconut, vinegar and vanilla; beat well by hand. Pour into pie shell. Bake at 350° for 40 minutes or until golden brown. Serve with whipped cream or vanilla ice cream.

Vicki Grant, Lynchburg
Montebello Camping & Fishing Resort

Blender Chocolate Fudge Pie

2 cups sugar
7 tablespoons cocoa
4 eggs
1¼ cups evaporated milk

1 tablespoon vanilla
1 stick margarine, melted
2 (8-inch) pie shells

Preheat oven to 350°. Combine first 6 ingredients in blender and mix well. Pour into pie shells and bake 35 to 40 minutes. Remove from oven while center is still shaky, and allow to set before cutting.

Deborah B. Borum
Blackstone Arts & Crafts Festival

Pork, Peanut & Pine Festival

Third week in July

Chippokes Plantation State Park
757-294-3625
www.porkpeanutpinefestival.org

The Pork, Peanut & Pine Festival began in 1976 as a project of the Surry County Bicentennial Committee. A core group of volunteers continues this tradition today honoring the crops of peanuts, corn, soybeans, wheat and cotton that have been the livelihood of Surry County since the 1600s.

Around 100 artisans and crafters are located throughout the gardens of Chippokes. Come and enjoy a family atmosphere filled with all types of food, from pork chops to chitterlings and funnel cakes to peanut pie. There is music on both days featuring bluegrass, country, gospel and pop. A parade is held on Saturday at noon, and visitors will not want to miss the BBQ cook-off. Other activities include working demonstrations and exhibits on pork products, peanut-growing, a working sawmill display, and old gas and steam engine exhibits.

Virginia Peanut Pie

Crust:

1⅓ cups flour teaspoon salt
½ cup shortening

1 egg, slightly beaten
2 teaspoon vinegar

Preheat oven to 350°. Combine flour and salt in mixing bowl. Cut in shortening with pastry blender or two knives until mixture is uniform. Add egg, vinegar and water. Toss lightly with fork. Work dough into firm ball. On lightly floured surface, roll dough into circle 1-inch larger than an inverted 9-inch pie pan. Gently lift dough into pan. Trim ½-inch beyond edge. Fold under to make double thickness around rim. Flute edge. Bake 12 minutes or until lightly browned.

Filling:

3 eggs, lightly beaten
½ cup white sugar
¾ cup light brown sugar, firmly
    packed
½ cup light corn syrup

½ teaspoon salt
1 teaspoon vanilla extract
6 tablespoons butter
1 cup chopped roasted peanuts

Combine lightly beaten eggs, sugars, corn syrup, salt, vanilla and butter in mixing bowl. Stir in peanuts and pour mixture into pie shell. Bake 45 minutes or until set. Cool and serve.

Eva Livesay
Pork, Peanut & Pine Festival

Apple Crisps

4 cups sliced apples (4 medium apples)
1 cup raisins
1 cup chopped walnuts
⅔ cup brown sugar

½ cup flour
½ cup oats
½ teaspoon cinnamon
½ teaspoon nutmeg
½ cup butter, softened

Preheat oven to 375°. Grease 8x8-inch pan. Place apples, raisins and walnuts in pan. Mix remaining ingredients thoroughly. Sprinkle over apples. Bake 30 minutes or until apples are tender and topping is golden brown.

Bettie Musso
General's Ridge Vineyard

Southern Pecan Tartlets

36 frozen mini phyllo shells
⅓ cup semi-sweet mini chocolate chips
1 cup chopped pecans
¾ cups firmly packed brown sugar
1 tablespoon butter, softened
1 large egg, lightly beaten
¼ cup bourbon

Preheat oven to 350°. Arrange shells on lightly greased jelly roll pan. Sprinkle chips in bottom of shells. In medium mixing bowl, stir together pecans, brown sugar, butter, egg and bourbon. Spoon evenly into shells. Bake 20 minutes or until golden brown. Store in airtight container.

Hunter House Victorian Museum

Aunt Bea's Quick Cobbler

Blackberries or peaches are great for this recipe, but any fresh fruit can be used.

Fruit Mixture:

4 cups sliced fruit
1 cup sugar

2 teaspoons cornstarch

Preheat oven to 325°. Combine all ingredients and set aside.

Crust:

¼ pound butter
1 cup flour
1 cup sugar

2 teaspoons baking powder
¾ cup milk

Melt butter in 9x13-inch pan. Mix remaining ingredients and pour over butter. Spoon fruit mixture on top of batter. Batter will rise while baking to form crust. Bake 1 hour.

Jackie Erickson
Ben Lomond

Easy Peach Cobbler

½ cup unsalted butter, melted
1 cup flour
2 cups sugar, divided
3 tablespoons baking powder
Pinch salt
1 cup milk
4 cups peeled, pitted and thinly sliced fresh peaches (5 to 6
   medium-size)
1 tablespoon fresh lemon juice
Ground cinnamon or ground nutmeg, optional

Preheat oven to 375°. Pour butter into 9x13-inch baking dish. In a medium bowl, combine flour, 1 cup sugar, baking powder and salt. Mix well. Stir in milk, mixing until just combined. Pour batter over butter but do not stir. In a small saucepan, combine peaches, lemon juice and remaining sugar. Bring to a boil over high heat, stirring constantly. Pour peaches over batter but do not stir. Sprinkle with cinnamon of nutmeg if desired. Bake 40 to 45 minutes or until top is golden-brown. May be served warm or cold.

Dori Sanders, author of Clover
Crossing at the Dan

Low-Carb Strawberry Rhubarb Cobbler

2 cups fresh rhubarb, cut into ½-inch
cubes
Juice and zest from 1 lemon
2 tablespoons maple syrup
2 tablespoons fresh orange juice
¼ teaspoon salt
3 cups sliced fresh strawberries

¼ cup whole wheat flour
¼ cup ground cornmeal
½ teaspoon cinnamon
¼ teaspoon ground ginger
2 tablespoons vegetable oil
2 tablespoons fat free buttermilk

Preheat oven to 350°. In a saucepan, combine rhubarb, lemon, maple syrup, orange juice and salt. Bring to a boil, reduce heat and simmer 10 minutes to soften rhubarb. Remove from heat and stir in strawberries. Divide mixture evenly among 8 (1-cup) ramekins. In a separate bowl, combine flour, cornmeal, cinnamon, ginger, oil and buttermilk (mixture should resemble wet sand). Divide crumble mixture evenly over ramekins. Bake 15 to 18 minutes or until crust is set and fruit mixture is bubbly. Cool 10 minutes before serving.

Chef Katie
Great Country Farms

Great Country Farms

18780 Foggy Bottom Road • Bluemont
540-554-2073 • www.greatcountryfarms.com

Great Country Farms is a 200 acre working farm situated at the base of the Blue Ridge Mountains outside the village of Bluemont. Great Country Farms offers produce as well as the farm experience to its customers. The Zurschmeide Family has been farming in Loudoun County for over 35 years and Great Country Farms was started by the second generation of Zurschmeides in Loudoun in 1994. In 1996 and again in 2007, the Loudoun County Chamber of Commerce voted Great Country Farms, "Agribusiness of the Year" for its unique efforts to farm in a difficult climate through innovation.

Great Country Farms has a ton of events and activities throughout the year. The Strawberry Jubilee, Father's Day Fish & Putt Putt, the BBQ & Blackberry Bonanza, Dog Days Peach Festival and Marshmallow Harvest are just a few of the fun celebrations. But it doesn't end there. There's a corn maze, fishing, hayrides, gem mining and an enormous outdoor pillow of air for jumping! Now THAT sounds like fun!

Visit their site for hours of operation, event dates and times.

Triple Ginger Squares

2½ cups flour
1 tablespoon baking powder
1 tablespoon ground ginger
2 teaspoons freshly grated ginger
1 teaspoon ground black pepper
1 teaspoon salt

1 cup unsalted butter, softened
1½ cups sugar
¼ cup honey
¼ cup mild-flavored molasses
2 large eggs
1 cup milk

Preheat oven to 350°. Butter and line 9x13-inch baking pan with parchment paper. Butter paper; set aside. In medium bowl combine flour, baking powder, ground ginger, fresh ginger, black pepper and salt; set aside. In a separate bowl, combine butter and sugar. Beat with mixer on medium speed until light and fluffy, about 2 minutes. With mixer on low, beat in honey and molasses until well incorporated. Beat in eggs. On low speed, beat flour mixture into sugar mixture in 3 additions, adding milk with each addition until combined. Pour batter to prepared baking pan. Bake in center of oven until toothpick inserted into center of cake comes out clean, 33 to 35 minutes. Remove from oven and cool 5 minutes. Invert cake and turn out on wire rack; remove paper. Invert again onto another rack set over waxed paper.

Cake Glaze:

3½ cups powdered sugar
5 tablespoons whipping cream
6 tablespoons unsalted butter
1 tablespoon mild-flavored molasses

10 pieces crystallized ginger, cut
    into 48 strips (buy ginger in strips
    or slices rather than nuggets)

Sift powdered sugar into medium bowl; set aside. In small saucepan, combine cream, butter and molasses over medium heat. Cook and stir until butter melts. Pour cream mixture into sugar and stir until smooth. Pour glaze over hot cake and, working quickly, spread evenly with spatula to cover top. Let stand at least 4 hours. With serrated knife dipped in hot water and wiped dry, cut cake into 24 squares, about 2x2 inches. Top each square with 2 ginger strips, crossed. Makes 24 servings.

Karen Solana
Herbs Galore & More at Maymont

Lemon Bars

Crust:

2 sticks unsalted butter, softened
2 cups flour

½ cup powdered sugar, plus
    additional for dusting

Preheat oven to 350°. Combine butter, flour and sugar and blend with electric mixer at medium speed (mixture will be crumbly). Press crumbs in bottom of ungreased 9x13-inch baking dish and bake 20 minutes. Cool slightly.

Filling:

4 eggs, beaten
2 cups sugar
½ cup lemon juice

¼ cup flour
1 teaspoon baking powder
Pinch salt

Combine eggs, sugar and lemon juice and blend with electric mixer at medium speed. Add flour, baking powder and salt and mix well. Pour lemon mixture over crust, return to oven and bake 25 minutes, until lightly browned. Cool completely. Sprinkle with powdered sugar and cut into squares.

Cheryl Kellert
Gray Ghost Vineyards

Gray Ghost Vineyards

Aunt Mignon's Brownies

⅓ cup butter
¼ cup sugar
2 tablespoons water
1½ cup chocolate chips, divided

1 teaspoon vanilla
3 eggs
¼ cup flour
¼ teaspoon baking soda

Preheat oven to 325°. Grease 9-inch square pan. Combine butter, sugar and water in saucepan and bring to boil. Remove from heat. Add 1 cup chocolate chips and vanilla. Stir until smooth. Add eggs, 1 at a time, stirring well. In separate bowl, combine flour and baking soda. Gradually blend into chocolate mixture. Stir in remaining chocolate chips. Spread in pan and bake 35 minutes. Cut when completely cool.

Occoquan Craft Fair

Chocolate Covered Butter Creams

1 pound butter, softened
2½ pounds powdered sugar
2 teaspoons vanilla
½ block paraffin
6 ounces unsweetened baking chocolate

Cream together butter, sugar and vanilla. Refrigerate until chilled. Roll into 1-inch balls. Melt paraffin and chocolate in double boiler. Using toothpicks, dip balls into chocolate mixture. Drain on waxed paper. Store in airtight container.

Hunter House Victorian Museum

Butterscotch Scotchies

1 package yellow cake mix
1 cup brown sugar
2 tablespoons butter, melted
2 tablespoons honey
2 tablespoons water

2 eggs, beaten
1 (12-ounce) package
  chocolate chips
Powdered sugar to taste

Preheat oven to 350°. Grease 11x13-inch pan. Combine all ingredients and mix well. Pour batter into pan. Bake 30 to 35 minutes. Cool in pan. Sprinkle with powdered sugar. Cut into bars to serve.

Hunter House Victorian Museum

Hunter House Victorian Museum

240 West Freemason Street • Norfolk
757-623-9814 • www.hunterhousemuseum.org

Located in Norfolk's Historic Freemason District is the Hunter House Victorian Museum. This 1894 Richardsonian Romanesque town home was designed and built for the successful merchant and banker, James W. Hunter and his family. The museum exhibits the family's collection of Victorian furnishings and decorative arts complemented with lavish reproduction papers and textiles. Tours for individuals or groups are available April through December. Afternoon teas and seasonal events are offered regularly throughout the year. Oktoberfest in September and the Olde World Christmas Market in November are fun introductions to the festive Christmas season. Visitors will have a lovely shopping experience in The Shop, Hunter House Victorian Museum gift store featuring stationery, books, specialty gifts and everything for tea, including their own signature blend, Miss Eloise's Afternoon Tea.

Cashew-Lemon Shortbread Cookies

½ cup roasted cashews
1 cup butter, softened
1 cup sugar, divided
Zest of 1 lemon

1 teaspoon vanilla
2 teaspoons lemon extract
2 cups flour

Place cashews in food processor and process fine. Add butter, ½ cup sugar, lemon zest, vanilla and lemon extract. Process till well blended. Add flour and use pulse action to blend and dough begins to form ball. Shape into 1½-inch balls and roll in remaining sugar. Place on ungreased cookie sheet 2 inches apart. Flatten with bottom of drinking glass. Bake at 325° for 17 minutes or until edges are lightly brown.

Lorri Amidon
Heathsville Farmers Market

Heathsville Farmers Market

Third Saturday of April thru October: 9am to 1pm

73 Monument Place • Heathsville
804-580-3377 • www.rhhtfoundation.org

Located in Historic Heathsville is Rice's Hotel/ Hughlett's Tavern, home of the Heathsville Farmers Market. Vendors come every third Saturday during the season to sell fresh produce, local honey, hand spun towels, carved wood spoons, forged items, native plants, brooms and handcrafted jewelry, providing great shopping for everyone. The Market hosts monthly events for kids and adults alike.

Call for more information about the Market or the Historic Rice's Hotel/Hughlett's Tavern.

Chocolate Chip Shortbread Cookies

2 cups real butter
2 cups plus 2 tablespoons powdered sugar
2 teaspoons vanilla
4½ cups flour
12 ounces semi-sweet miniature chocolate chips

Preheat oven to 350°. Cream butter and 2 cups powdered sugar. Beat in vanilla. Gradually add flour until well blended. Stir in chocolate chips. Dough will be very stiff. Shape into 1-inch balls. Place on ungreased cookie sheet. Flatten with a fork. Bake 15 minutes. While warm, sprinkle tops with powdered sugar.

Hunter House Victorian Museum

Lavender Cookies

½ cup shortening
½ cup butter, softened
1¼ cups sugar
2 eggs
1 teaspoon vanilla extract
½ teaspoon almond extract

2¼ cups flour
4 teaspoons culinary lavender
  buds
1 teaspoon baking powder
½ teaspoon salt

Cream together shortening, butter and sugar. Add eggs, beating well. Blend in extracts. In separate bowl, combine dry ingredients and gradually add to wet mixture. Drop by rounded teaspoons on lightly greased cookie sheet. Bake at 350° for 8 to 10 minutes or until golden brown.

White Oak Lavender Farm

Molasses Crinkle Cookies

½ cup soft shortening
1 cup brown sugar
1 egg
¼ cup Grandma's Original Molasses
2¼ cups sifted flour

1 teaspoon baking soda
¼ teaspoon salt
1 teaspoon ground cinnamon
1 teaspoon ground ginger
White sugar for topping

Combine shortening, brown sugar, egg and molasses and blend thoroughly with electric mixer. Sift together flour, baking soda, salt, cinnamon and ginger; add to batter, stirring with spoon. Cover bowl with plastic wrap and refrigerate 2 to 24 hours. Roll dough into walnut-size balls. Dip tops in sugar. Place sugared side up, 3 inches apart on parchment paper lined baking sheet. Sprinkle each cookie with 2 or 3 drops water to produce crackled surface. Bake at 350° for 10 to 12 minutes.

Ellen Arnold, Volunteer
O. Winston Link Museum

O. Winston Link Museum

101 Shenandoah Avenue • Roanoke
540-982-5465 • www.linkmuseum.org

From 1955 to 1960, Brooklyn photographer O. Winston Link traveled, photographing and documenting the end of the steam locomotive era on the Norfolk and Western Railway—the last major line to exclusively operate under steam power. During those five years, Link captured more than 2,400 images. The O. Winston Link Museum exhibits this body of work as well as the history of the N&W Railway. Artifacts, films and interactive displays complement more than 250 dramatic black and white and color photographs taken throughout the mountains of Virginia, West Virginia, Maryland, and

North Carolina. Stop by and meet the people in the locomotive shops, on the trains, and along the lines in a 1950s world now vanished from our landscape. Return to a bygone era of steam through Link's stunning photographs, films, and sound recordings.

Belgian Beer Cookies

2 (12-ounce) bottles Belgian-style
   white beer
5 tablespoons honey
1½ sticks unsalted butter,
   softened
1¼ cups powdered sugar

1 egg
½ teaspoon vanilla extract
1 orange, zested
2 teaspoons ground coriander
2 cups flour
½ teaspoon baking soda

Preheat oven to 350°. Put beer and honey in medium saucepan and reduce over medium heat until there is ⅓ cup liquid, skimming foam off occasionally. Allow liquid to cool to room temperature. Combine butter and sugar; blend well with electric mixer. Add egg and mix thoroughly. Add vanilla, orange zest, coriander, and beer mixture; blend. In a separate bowl, mix flour and baking soda together and slowly add to batter. Place batter in rounded tablespoons on aluminum cookie sheet lined with parchment paper. Bake for 18 to 20 minutes.

Chef Randall Spencer
Blue Ridge Mountain Catering
Blacksburg Fork and Cork

Italian Ricotta Cookies

2 sticks butter, softened
1 cup Ricotta cheese
2 teaspoons vanilla extract
2 cups sugar

2 eggs
4 cups flour
1 teaspoon baking soda
1 teaspoon salt

Preheat oven to 350°. Combine butter and Ricotta, blend until creamy. Add vanilla; mix well. Add sugar gradually. Add eggs and mix well. Slowly stir in dry ingredients and blend well. Drop dough in rounded teaspoons onto greased cookie sheet. Bake 10 to 12 minutes.

Brenda Wrightington
Representative for Italy, International Children's Festival

International Children's Festival

Third Saturday in April

Mill Point Park • Hampton
757-727-8314
www.hampton.gov/parks/icf

Imagine 15,000 people all gathered together in a beautiful park setting in downtown Hampton, each one taking in the sights, sounds, and tastes of cultures from across the globe. Each year, over thirty-five countries are represented at the International Children's Festival, a veritable ocean of color, cultural pride and camaraderie. The day begins with the Parade of Nations, each participant proudly displaying the ornate native garbs of their homeland. The enticing smells of

food from distant lands waft over the festival, as ethnic food vendors line the park greeting visitors and festival attendees alike. The festival boasts entertainment on three stages throughout the day, as well as roaming entertainment. In 2009, ICF welcomed school groups from as far away as Chicago nationally, and Korea internationally, to celebrate this educationally unique and entertaining event. Families will have a blast traveling the world in Downtown Hampton.

Christmas Cookies

1 cup butter
1 cup white sugar
½ cup brown sugar
3 eggs
3 cups flour
Pinch salt
1 teaspoon cinnamon
1 teaspoon cloves
1 teaspoon baking soda

2 tablespoons hot water
½ cup chopped candied
  pineapple
1 pound dates, chopped
1 pound raisins
1 cup chopped pecans
1 cup chopped walnuts
1 cup chopped black walnuts

Combine butter, sugars and eggs; mix well. In separate bowl, sift together flour, salt, cinnamon and cloves. Add dry mixture to butter mixture and stir well. Dissolve baking soda in water and add to batter. Add pineapple, dates, raisins and nuts. Drop by rounded spoonfuls onto baking sheet. Bake at 325° for 10 minutes.

Margrate Dye
Richlands Fall Festival

Christmas Cookies

½ cup melted butter
1 egg
1 teaspoon vanilla extract
1 cup white chocolate chips
1 cup cranberries
1 cup oatmeal

¾ cup flour
½ cup brown sugar
½ cup white sugar
½ teaspoon baking soda
½ teaspoon salt

Preheat oven to 375°. Combine all ingredients. Chill, covered, 30 minutes. Drop by tablespoon on ungreased cookie sheet and bake 8 to 10 minutes.

Margaret Staton
Virginia Southern Gospel Jubilee

Preacher Cookies

Preacher cookies were given their name because if you see the preacher walking down your lane, you can have these cookies prepared by the time he reaches your door.

½ cup butter, softened
4 tablespoons unsweetened
   cocoa powder
2 cups sugar
½ cup milk
½ teaspoon salt

3 cups quick cooking oats
½ cup peanut butter
1 teaspoon vanilla extract
½ cup coconut, optional
½ cup nuts, optional

Mix butter, cocoa, sugar, milk, and salt together in saucepan. Bring to rolling boil; cook 1 minute. Remove from heat. Stir in oatmeal, peanut butter, vanilla, coconut and nuts. Drop by tablespoonfuls onto waxed paper. Allow to cool completely and harden.

Reynolds Homestead

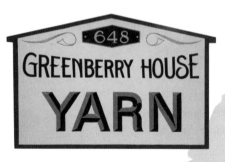

Greenberry House

648 Concord Road • Meadows of Dan
½ mile outside Meadows of Dan
276-952-2444

A specialty yarn and spinning shop offering hand dyed and hand spun yarns, spinning and felting fiber from local and regional artisans and farmers. Demonstrations daily in the on-site artisan studio and space available for dyeing and crafting by visitors. The shop also features fine and antiquarian books and paper collectibles, along with unique knitting notions and spinning supplies.

Grandpa's Wild Blackberry Dumplings

2½ cups ripe wild blackberries, divided
⅔ cup sugar

1 cup water
2¼ cups Bisquick
⅔ cup milk

Bring 2 cups blackberries, sugar, and water to boil in a large saucepan. Boil 5 minutes. In a separate bowl, combine Bisquick and milk, stirring well. Drop dumpling mixture into boiling blackberries with large spoon. (Be careful not to splash boiling syrup.) Add remaining blackberries. Reduce heat, cover and simmer 20 minutes. Delicious served with cream, ice cream or Cool Whip.

Greenberry House
Mountain Meadow Farm

Mountain Meadow Farm

"Corn Acoustics!" Corn Maze • Sue's Pumpkin Patch
84 Concord Road • Meadows of Dan
Just 150 yards off the Blue Ridge Parkway and 50 yards from Business 58
276-952-5568 • www.mountainmeadowcrafts.com

Every September through the end of October Mountain Meadow Farm provides family fun with a themed six acre Corn Maze. Located in a lovely agri-tourism community, the Corn Maze highlights the heritage music of beautiful Southwest Virginia. Adding a new experience for visitors is Sue's "Pick Your Own Fun" Pumpkin Patch. Five festivals, beginning in May, are held throughout the season at the Corn Maze site. Visit the web site for more information on these events.

In addition, the busy farm offers wonderful home grown vegetables straight from the garden at Mountain Meadow Farm and Craft Market, a unique craft and farmers' market offering authentic handmade quality crafts produced by local artisans.

Corn Maze from above

The mission statement: Uniting Southwestern Virginia's Artisans and Craftsmen With Local Heritage Farmers to Preserve the Traditions of Days Gone By. Come experience the fun!

Peach Dumplings

2 cans crescent dinner rolls
6 to 8 peaches, washed, peeled and sliced
2 sticks melted butter
1½ cups sugar
1 teaspoon cinnamon
1 (12-ounce) can Sprite

Separate crescent rolls. Wrap 1 peach slice with a crescent roll, beginning with wide end. Place in 9x13-inch pan. Scatter remaining peaches around crescent rolls. In a medium size bowl, combine butter, sugar and cinnamon. Pour over crescent rolls. Pour Sprite over entire pan. Bake at 350° for 30 minutes or until golden brown.

Shirley Keene
Virginia State Peach Festival

Abingdon Medical Museum

Peaches 'n Cream

½ cup self-rising flour
6 tablespoons butter, melted
6 eggs
2 small packages vanilla instant pudding mix
1 cup milk
2 (32-ounce) cans peaches, drained (reserve juice)

2 (8-ounce) packages cream cheese, softened
6 tablespoons peach juice (reserved juice)
1⅛ cup sugar, divided
½ teaspoon cinnamon

Preheat oven to 350°. Combine flour, butter, eggs, pudding mix and milk. Mix well. Spread into greased glass baking dish. Spread peaches over batter. In separate bowl, combine cream cheese, peach juice and 1 cup sugar; blend until smooth. Spread over peaches. Sprinkle with remaining sugar and cinnamon. Bake 30 minutes.

Tressia Boyd
Richlands Fall Festival

Date Crackers

1 can sweetened condensed milk
1 cup chopped dates
1 cup chopped pecans
1 box Ritz crackers

Preheat oven to 250°. Heat milk and dates over medium heat until thick; stir in nuts and spread 1 teaspoon mixture on each cracker. Place on baking sheet and bake 5 minutes.

Topping:
¾ block cream cheese, softened
2 cups powdered sugar
½ teaspoon vanilla extract

Combine all ingredients. Spoon 1 teaspoon onto cooled crackers.

Beverly Viers
Wise County Famous Fall Fling

Dutch Babies

½ cup butter
6 eggs

1½ cups flour
1½ cups milk

Preheat oven to 425°. Melt butter in oven-proof skillet. In separate bowl, combine eggs, flour and milk. Blend until slightly lumpy. Pour into skillet. Bake 20 to 25 minutes. Serve with powdered sugar or fruit.

Occoquan Craft Fair

Praline Pumpkin Dessert

1 (15-ounce) can pumpkin
1 (12-ounce) can evaporated milk
3 eggs
1 cup sugar
4 teaspoons pumpkin pie spice

1 box yellow cake mix
1½ cups chopped pecans
¾ cup butter, melted
Whipped cream, optional

Preheat oven to 350°. Grease and flour a 9x13-inch baking dish. In a medium bowl, beat pumpkin, milk, eggs, sugar and pumpkin pie spice with wire whisk until smooth. Pour into pan. Sprinkle dry cake mix over pumpkin mixture. Sprinkle with pecans and pour melted butter evenly over top. Bake 50 to 60 minutes or until knife inserted in center comes out clean. Cool 30 minutes. Serve with a dollop of whipped cream.

Culpeper Air Fest

Culpeper Air Fest
Second Saturday in October

Culpeper Regional Airport
12517 Beverly Ford Road
Brandy Station
540-825-8280
www.culpeperairport.com

Look skyward for the Annual Culpeper Air Fest! This day long event is free for the entire family, thanks to their generous sponsors Terremark, Chemung, Cedar Mountain Stone and Eurocomposites. Attendees have the opportunity to get up close to fantastic aircraft of all types and visit with the pilots before these planes take to the air. Stunt pilots, the Bealton Flying Circus, vintage planes flying in formation, and the only civilian-owned Harrier in the world will decorate the sky and amaze the crowd. There is always plenty of food, refreshments and more.

Culpeper Airport is conveniently located off Route 29 in Brandy Station. Parking is available with shuttle service.

Raspberry Dessert

Crust:
1 cup flour
1 stick butter, melted
½ cup ground pecans

Combine flour, butter and pecans. Pat into 9x13-inch baking dish. Bake at 350° for 10 minutes or until lightly brown.

Filling:
1 (8-ounce) package cream cheese, softened
⅓ cup lemon juice
1 can sweetened condensed milk
½ teaspoon vanilla extract

Combine all ingredients and spread on cooled crust.

Topping:
16 ounces raspberries
2 tablespoons gelatin in water
½ cup sugar
1 cup whipping cream

Combine fruit and gelatin; spread on cream cheese mixture. Mix sugar and whipping cream. Spread on fruit mixture. Cover and chill 3 hours.

Culpeper Air Fest

Huckleberry Dessert

2 cups graham cracker crumbs
⅓ cup butter, melted
2 tablespoons sugar
1 (8-ounce) cream cheese, softened
1 (8-ounce) carton Cool Whip
32 ounces Huckleberry Pie Filling by The Country Canner

Combine first 3 ingredients and press into a 9x13-inch pan; set aside. Blend cream cheese and Cool Whip together and spread into pan over cracker crumbs. Pour pie filling in over top and chill.

The Country Canner

The Country Canner

Homemade Rock Candy

1 cup water	1 pencil
2 cups sugar, plus additional for cooking	Length of cord
	Glass jar

Put water and sugar into small saucepan. Heat over medium heat, stirring continually, until sugar melts. Continue adding sugar until it will no longer dissolve in the water (there will be sugar lying in bottom of pan). Remove from heat and let cool until just warm. Pour into glass jar. Tie 1 end of a heavy cord to middle of a pencil. Place pencil over jar opening, allowing cord to fall into liquid. Crystals will begin to form on cord in a few hours. The next day, remove pencil and cord from jar; set aside. Pour liquid into pan, reheat, pour and cool as done previously. Reinsert cord with the crystals on it. More crystals will form. As this procedure is repeated, larger crystals will form. Once crystals are desired size, snip and enjoy.

Grand Caverns Staff
Grand Caverns

Grand Caverns

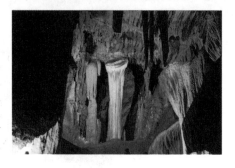

5 Grand Caverns Drive • Grottoe
888-430-CAVE (2283)
www.grandcaverns.com

Grand Caverns, owned by the Town of Grottoes, is America's oldest continuously operated show cave, voted #2 in America by Parade magazine and a National Natural Landmark. Grand Caverns is a prime example of history and beauty. With an abundance of rare shield formations and history around every turn, visitors can see why it is "Grand." Guests receive personal service and enjoy the wonders of an underground marvel.

Grand Caverns hosts the annual Heritage Day Festival in June celebrating the area's rich heritage with living history exhibits and demonstrations. The day also offers a candlelight tour and authentic ball in the Grand Ballroom in the evening. The Caverns also hosts the annual Bluegrass in the Park Festival every September, which benefits the Shriner's Children's Hospital. Also in September is the Harvest Festival on Main Street featuring craft and food vendors and entertainment throughout the day. Grand Caverns is also a Civil War Trails Attraction, with opportunities to hike, bike, fish, play mini-golf, and swim in season in a beautiful park setting.

Aunt Myrtle's Peanut Butter Fudge

2 cups brown sugar
2 cups white sugar
¼ pound butter
1 cup evaporated milk
1 cup peanut butter
1 teaspoon vanilla

Cook sugars, butter and evaporated milk till soft ball forms in cold water. Add peanut butter. Cool some, then beat and add vanilla. Beat until batter stiffens but is still pourable. Put in 7x11-inch pan. Cut when cool.

Sandee Burt, Moneta
Smith Mountain Lake

Peanut Butter Fudge Candy

1½ cups sugar
7 tablespoons milk
1 tablespoon corn syrup
4 tablespoons butter

2 squares semi-sweet chocolate
1 teaspoon vanilla extract
⅓ cup peanut butter

Combine sugar, milk, corn syrup, butter and chocolate in a heavy 2 quart saucepan. Cook over high heat, stirring constantly, until chocolate melts and all is boiling. Reduce heat to low and cook 2 minutes, stirring constantly. Remove from heat and stir in vanilla and peanut butter. Continue stirring until mixture thickens. While still warm, pour into greased 7x10-inch or 9x9-inch pan. Cool 1 hour. Cut into 1-inch squares.

Ellen Arnold, Volunteer
O. Winston Link Museum

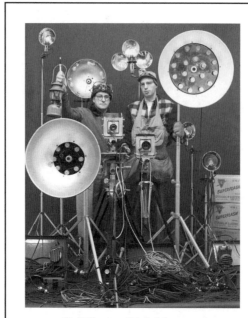

O. Winston Link Museum

Index

Virginia State Flower
Cornus florida

Index of Events & Destinations

This Index is meant to be a tool for locating all events and destinations featured in *Eat & Explore Virginia*. Each event or destination is listed by both name and city referencing the page number for its featured page. Events and destinations that have a recipe are additionally listed by event or destination name then recipe, referencing the page number for the recipe. A complete Index of Recipes begins on page 255.

Index of Recipes

P

Recipe Notes

Travel Plans

About the Author:

In 1999, Christy Campbell began her journey in the world of cookbooks when she took a position at a publishing company specializing in regional cookbooks. At the time, it was an all-new experience, so she immersed herself in cookbooks, both at home and at the office. With the help of the associate publisher and her personal mentor, Sheila Simmons (author, STATE HOMETOWN COOKBOOK SERIES), Christy learned the in's and out's of the small press world, devoting herself to cookbooks for the next 6 years. After the birth of her youngest son, Campbell took a sabbatical from the publishing world to focus on her young family.

In 2009, Campbell reconnected with Sheila Simmons and began work with Great American Publishers, reenergizing a 10 year love of cookbooks. She is now an integral part of Great American Publishers and has begun a new cookbook series of her own. The EAT & EXPLORE STATE COOKBOOK SERIES chronicles the favorite recipes of local cooks across the United States while highlighting the most popular events and destinations in each state.

When she is not writing cookbooks, selling cookbooks or cooking recipes for cookbooks, Christy Campbell enjoys volunteering at her children's school, running and reading. She lives in Brandon, Mississippi, with her husband Michael and their two sons.

State Hometown Cookbook Series
A Hometown Taste of America, One State at a Time

EACH: **$18.95 • 240 to 272 pages • 8x9 • paperbound**

The STATE HOMETOWN COOKBOOK SERIES captures each state's hometown charm by combining great-tasting local recipes from real hometown cooks with interesting stories and photos from festivals all over the state. As a souvenir, gift, or collector's item, this unique series is sure to take you back to your hometown... or take you on a journey to explore other hometowns across the country.

Georgia Hometown Cookbook
978-1-934817-01-8 (1-934817-01-5)

Louisiana Hometown Cookbook
978-1-934817-07-0 (1-934817-07-4)

Mississippi Hometown Cookbook
978-1-934817-08-7 (1-934817-08-2)

Tennessee Hometown Cookbook
978-0-9779053-2-4 (0-9779053-2-2)

Texas Hometown Cookbook
978-1-934817-04-9 (1-934817-04-X)

• Easy to follow recipes produce great-tasting dishes every time.

• Recipes use ingredients you probably already have in your pantry.

• Fun-to-read sidebars feature food-related festivals across the state.

• The perfect gift for anyone who loves to cook.

• Makes a great souvenir.

292 Recipes for 30 Varieties of Wild Game

Respected hunter and chef Harold Webster shares 300 of his personal favorite recipes in his latest cookbook. As readers have come to expect, Webster's recipes are so easy to use that even a novice cook will be at home in kitchen yet interesting enough challenge the most experienced chef. In addition to the recipes, Webster tells fascinating stories about the capturing, cleaning and cooking of the game. Making this book an entertaining read as well as an essential resource for creating memorable meals from any hunter's Bounty.

$16.95 • 240 pp • 7 x 10 • paperbound • 978-0-9779053-1-7

www.GreatAmericanPublishers.com • www.facebook.com/GreatAmericanPublishers

Eat & Explore Cookbook Series

EAT AND EXPLORE STATE COOKBOOK SERIES is a favorite of local cooks, armchair travelers and cookbook collectors across the United States. Call us toll-free **1.888.854.5954** *to order additional copies or to join our Cookbook Club.*

EACH: **$18.95 • 240 to 272 pages • 7x9 • paperbound**

Now Available...   ## Coming Soon...

Virginia   ### Arkansas   ### Oklahoma   ### Minnesota   ### Washington

978-1-934817-12-4   978-1-934817-09-4   978-1-934817-11-7

Don't miss out on our upcoming titles—join our Cookbook Club and you'll be notified of each new edition.

www.GreatAmericanPublishers.com • www.facebook.com/GreatAmericanPublishers